The New Frontiers of Aging

THE NEW
FRONTIERS
OF AGING

Edited by
Wilma Donahue and
Clark Tibbitts

The University of Michigan Press
Ann Arbor

PREFACE

EACH YEAR, since 1948, the Division of Gerontology of the Institute for Human Adjustment and the Extension Service have co-operated in planning and offering a University of Michigan Conference on Aging.

The eighth conference, which was held in the summer of 1955, was entitled "Aging—Applying Today's Knowledge Today." Its purpose was to give recognition to the fact that much is already known which, if applied, would greatly improve the welfare of older persons.

In order to ensure a more comprehensive consideration of the various aspects of the processes and problems of aging, the University invited the cosponsorship of such federal agencies as the Department of Health, Education, and Welfare, the Department of Labor, the Civil Service Commission, and the Housing and Home Finance Agency; of the state Departments of Health, Mental Health, Agriculture, Public Instruction, Social Welfare, and Employment Security; and of the United Auto Workers Congress of Industrial Organizations, and the Michigan State Medical Society. The cosponsors took part in the planning of the conference and assigned many of their professional staff members to serve as resource personnel in the various parts of the conference program. The excellence of the

program was in large measure the result of the generous participation of these distinguished groups.

The conference program consisted of three types of sessions. The general sessions provided discussions of urgent contemporary problems resulting from the aging of the population and the development of new technological procedures. Eighteen workshops, the second type of session, were under the direction of nationally known authorities, who had the able assistance of resource persons in the problems under consideration. The workshops offered opportunity for an intensive study of the results of investigations and the application of practices in the fields of employment, housing, community organization, health, religion, education, use of leisure time, and legislative action and planning. The third phase of the program was a research symposium at which approximately twenty-five distinguished scientists pooled their knowledge for the purpose of identifying emerging concepts and principles and of pressing unanswered questions in the field of aging.

This book on *The New Frontiers of Aging* is devoted largely to a report of the research symposium. It offers one of the first correlated compilations of the trends and factors identified from data collected in original studies of the social problems of aging. Such information is of paramount importance to the understanding of the phenomenon of aging and to the development of good plans and social policies to meet the needs of older people.

It is a great loss to the reader that it is not possible to include in this book a report of the excellent discussions held by the various workshop groups. From the work of these groups it is apparent that progress is taking place in every aspect of the field of aging and that the lion's share of credit belongs to no single discipline or group of individuals. Aging is everybody's business and, as such, there is evidence that it is not being neglected. Continual gains of the same magnitude will not be maintained, however, unless the frontiers of knowledge are apprehended and the new trends and issues are used as the basis for advanced planning. It is, therefore, with great pleasure that the editors of this book present the concepts and principles which have emerged from research and systematic observation and raise some of the important questions of the day which remain to be investigated.

A special expression of appreciation is offered to McGregor Fund of Detroit, which provided a grant in support of the research symposium, and to Dr. Frank Sladen for his enthusiastic support of this program.

WILMA DONAHUE
CLARK TIBBITTS

CONTENTS

Beginning with Today's Knowledge

Part 1

INTRODUCTION *Chapter I*

THE REVEREND CANON EDWARD B. FERGUSON

> *The Reverend Canon Edward B. Ferguson is the director of the Department of Christian Social Relations of the Diocese of California (Episcopal). He was formerly executive secretary of the E. D. Farmer Foundation in Dallas, Texas.*

"APPLYING TODAY'S KNOWLEDGE TODAY" is an intriguing theme, perhaps because the emphasis is pragmatic and is concerned more with results than with theory. Such a title carries a dual premise: that today's knowledge is somehow different from yesterday's, and that time is important in the determination of our actions on the basis of our present knowledge.

Is today's knowledge about aging really different from the ancient wisdom of the race on the subject? I think that it is and that it differs not only because we have improved our means of observing facts about aging and our techniques for action on the basis of conclusions adduced from these facts, but also because the facts themselves have changed, both absolutely and relatively to their settings. And this is no mere increase in the quantity of knowledge; impressive as is the amount of change, more impressive still is the shift in kind of knowledge, which is so great as to mean a radical shift in our philosophy of aging. Although some declare that older people are inflexible, intractable, and unteachable, predisposed to unreasonable childishness, predominantly unemployable, and generally a burden to their communities, their families, and themselves, we are now in a position to challenge all of these assumptions, on the basis of demonstrable facts. While any of these assumptions may be true in individual cases, there is none among them which is an unquestionable function of aging; the lag in our cultural assimilation of new knowledge, however, contributes to the pressures for general acceptance of these false stereotypes.

The facts of aging in 1955 are different from those of 1855, of 1905, and even of 1945. To think of "applying today's knowledge today" carries the implication not only that time is important—that tomorrow may be too late—but also that yesterday's knowledge is not merely incomplete but potentially destructive of what we seek to accomplish. Surely, it was one who had experienced tragically belated action who observed: "Social reform is the process of creating the social problems of tomorrow by measures designed to solve the social problems of today." We would do just that if we were to continue using the standard methodologies of yesterday to deal with the problems of aging today. The field of concern for children offers a stern object lesson. At the turn of the century, when interest in the field of child welfare services was at a stage fairly comparable to that now becoming manifest in aging, a tremendous number of large congregate care institutions came into being. These institutions, although they were useful and perhaps not inappropriate to the problems of the nineteenth century, are now millstones round the neck in the twentieth century. Yesterday's knowledge is not adequate to meet today's challenge.

Basic to all our thinking shall be an undergirding philosophy: that the presence of vastly increased numbers of older people need not be an intolerable burden, but may be rather the greatest asset, and certainly the most stimulating challenge to the resourcefulness of all. Today we know the problems, we know some of the solutions, our task is to bring to bear those facts, techniques, and philosophies which will help older people to enjoy the fruits of the new America.

Preparation for Retirement

We are deeply concerned with the problems of employment of older people. These are problems not only because maintenance of money income is of primary concern to us in a money-based economy but also because employment has so many other meanings than those to which we may assign a dollar value. We know, for instance, that employment means not only income but status both within and without the family group and can mean to a person the crucial difference between healthy self-esteem and deprecatory depression. We know that fixed-age retirement is an industrial policy of questionable value. For reasons that are now relatively unamenable to immediate change, fixed-age retirement is likely to persist as a dominant pattern for quite some time. Therefore, it is of great practical value that we be concerned with preparation of employees for retirement at a fixed age. It is manifestly very late indeed to begin a retirement counseling program for an employee at the time the farewell watch, complete with epitaph, is given to him.

Is five years earlier also too late? Or ten? Many large companies now begin the process at the time of first employment. What might be the responsibilities of public and private educational facilities in these matters? What of the smaller businesses, whose managers have the will but lack the manpower and means to mount a full-scale retirement counseling service? At least one well-documented plan proposed an independent service, available on a graduated fee basis according to use, as a means of filling this serious need. Again, we know that there should be opportunity for gainful employment for all who desire work and are capable of it and that it has long since been demonstrated that older people can perform profitably to themselves and their employers when suitably placed. We know some, though by no means all, of the selection criteria for older workers and many of the proven techniques of such placement. Yet there is no urban area in this country which does not have its significant number of able older men and women who are "idle in the market-place . . . because no man hath hired us."

Health Needs of Older People

The health needs of older people present major problems the country over. Less than a third of them have insurance provision to meet the costs of medical care after their seventy-fifth year. In state after state, mental hospital facilities become more and more crowded with admissions of older people who do not really need long-term psychiatric care. Yet, unless this trend is modified swiftly, the healing services of many of these excellent hospitals will become hopelessly clogged with older people whose real needs could be more constructively met in their home communities with resources which already exist or can be developed relatively easily and inexpensively. We cannot afford the expenditure either of our financial or our social capital for hospitalizing people whose primary lack is expressible in terms of "a place in the sun . . . each under his own fig-tree and vine."

Community Resources Available

There is no community in this country which lacks the resources to do its own job of fact-finding, at least, with a minimal amount of consultative help. There will never be enough "experts" to do the fact-finding job for us, and it is distinctly questionable whether the use of them for this purpose would be sound, even if they were available. Saul Alinsky's quotation is one well worth nailing to the door of every town hall, every neighborhood center, every church in the land: "There is in *every* community, every neighborhood, enough indigenous leadership to guide the group as far as it is prepared to go." And there is virtually no community which lacks the resources to help immeasurably its older citizens to realize their tremendous potentialities.

Recreation Needs

All too frequently we are overcome and immobilized by the temptation to "sigh for what is not." As an example, improved social and recreational services for older people are an almost invariable critical need in American communities. The community that waits impatiently for some local benefactor to leave an impressive recreational building as his monument may wait in vain, and, in addition, it may experience the worse fate of believing that the existence of a physical facility has solved the problem. Recreation for older people is concerned with people, not with buildings, not with the quality or quantity of potholders produced by this person or that, but with the process by which there is set free, within the social group, the power by which the members may grow into themselves by growing out.

Responsibility of the Church

There is a great ground swell of interest in aging now stirring the church congregations of our country. Belatedly, the church is awakening to the conviction that the older people represent a neglected missionary frontier at her very doorstep. Many of these people have been inarticulately waiting in quiet desperation for their reintegration into the "redeeming fellowship." Many national and local churches are feverishly embarking upon ambitious institutional housing plans centered on the health and living security of their older people. Some of these plans, indeed, are well conceived and soundly based. But there are unfortunately many for whom Margaret Wagner's warning is appropriate: "We make great point of our efforts to 'make our elders comfortable'—and what we are really doing is making ourselves comfortable about them."

False Conceptions of Aging

Among the most dominant features of our time are gadgets and conformity. The current American *credo* apparently has as its basis the conviction that with enough inanimate "things" we can achieve the good life—particularly if no one dissents from the majority pattern. But there can never be enough things to satisfy the demand for them. Certainly, in our lifetimes there will not be enough with which to attack decisively the problems of older people. The remedy is an old one: improvisation, flexibility, the will-to-do which does not wait for tomorrow's wisdom, but strives today to apply today's knowledge.

We are still victims of the pressure to conform in our thinking about older people. The false stereotypes of aging are so engrained as to be plausible even to the aging who are the victims. The reason and the remedy are not far to seek: we reject age because we fear its outward signs, misreading and distorting them, twisting the meaning until objective evil is the result. And the remedy is a healthy iconoclasm, which refuses to be overwhelmed by mere numbers of custom:

Long ago, Fra Giovanni observed,

> "Life is so generous a giver, but we,
> Judging its gifts by their covering,
> Cast them away as ugly, or heavy, or hard.
> Remove the covering, and you will find beneath it
> A living splendor,
> Woven of love, by wisdom, with power."

AUTOMATION

PREDICTS CHANGE *Chapter II*

1. For the Older Worker

WARNER BLOOMBERG, JR.

Warner Bloomberg, Jr. is on the staff of the University of Chicago, where, for the past several years, he has taught survey courses in "Culture and Personality" and "American Political and Economic Institutions."

THE TEXTILE WORKERS' UNION has a song about the employee who passes on to his just reward in Paradise. The chorus of the ballad describes heaven as a factory where

> The walls were made out of marble,
> The machines were made out of gold;
> And nobody ever got tired,
> And nobody ever grew old.

Whether or not it seems contrived, this whimsical notion represents a reverse image of some of the industrial laborers' most deep-seated fears. They are fears which have become entrenched in our working class subcultures during two centuries of experience with factory production.

What is mirrored here is neither a distaste for work nor a yearning for an Eden of endless leisure. It is a revulsion against the kind of labor which leaves almost nothing of the worker's time and spirit for activities outside the mill and which contributes to an old age of weakness, rapid decay, and premature death. The image of debilitating old

age has been even more threatening to the worker than
has that of endlessly recurring weariness. To be unable to
carry on the factory job in times past was not only to be
thrown out on the dole of family or charity, it also was to
be robbed of that power over things which the worker has
through his part in the productive processes. This power is
central to the millhand's image of himself, to his identity,
although many of us who deal mainly with the intangibles
of abstractions or interpersonal relationships do not adequately understand it.

Vast improvements in the character and conditions of
industrial work have been and continue to be made as a
consequence of technological change, union programs, and
a more enlightened and sophisticated management. The
fears persist for some time, however, after the institutional
facts have altered, as a kind of cultural after-image which
affects the view of things that the worker, especially the
older worker, has. These fears continue to provide motivation for more demands with respect to pensions, seniority,
and job security.

Old-timers still tell newcomers to the plant how it was
in "the good old days" when they were first hired: how
they came out shaking after a turn in the hot mill or on
the assembly line; how a young man with wife and children might have little time or energy for anything but
eating and sleeping when he got home; how only the intensity of drinking, fighting, and sex could erase even
momentarily the hangover feelings from a long and arduous week in the shop. During the two-month steel strike
for pensions in 1952, the meetings at which United Steel-
workers' president Philip Murray spoke were generally
unemotional except at a few points. One of these was when
he asserted that the company had no right to "use up" a
workingman as if he were a mechanical device to be cast

on the junk heap when it wore out. "We are not machines," Murray said in his soft Scotch brogue, "we are men, created in the image of God." The millhands shook the auditorium with their approving roar.

Reasons for Demotion of Older Workers

Even today old age, like weariness, can be a form of defeat. For many years a steelworker—call him "Fred"—was a fine craneman. But a few years ago Fred failed to pass the eyesight exam for crane operators even when wearing glasses. The only other job of equivalent status in his department was a task far too arduous for most men in their fifties; after a few weeks of trying it Fred was showing signs of real exhaustion. To remain in the mill he would have had to move down the pay-skill-status ladder into a laboring job such as sweeping the floor, or perhaps he could "hook" with the crane, a few notches above labor. At this point the company offered to hire him as a guard and he took this job, even though becoming part of the plant protection force meant loss of his status as a production employee with its accumulated union membership benefits.

The sudden demotion of old-timers has been a result also of technological change which, like the decline of physical abilities, usually hits hardest at those who have spent their lives in the mill, men who have acquired skills that one new installation can make useless. As one employee said: "There are guys walking around here with shovels and brooms who had more know-how in their right hand than most of us'll gain in a lifetime, but the machines they ran went out the door on the scrap truck."

Pattern of Life Among Industrial Workers

Here, then, has been a common pattern of life among the industrial workers of preceding and, to a degree, present generations. During his prime a millhand might rise above the subsistence level which likely characterized his existence as a child in a large and inadequately supported family. Then marriage and procreative fruitfulness, technological change, and his own declining powers combine to drag him back down. With age and demotion or loss of work there could all too easily come a time when even the subsistence level might look rather like paradise.

Rise of Automatic Production

An increase of production during past times depended in part upon making the men work ever faster, for in each stage of production workers were pitted against the "hardness of the material," either directly or with the aid of tools or machinery. The worker wove the material, or shaped it, or cut it, or cast it, or hammered on it, or fitted one piece together with another. Slowly the tools and the machinery —the ratchet-type screwdriver, the semiautomatic lathe— were made more automatic. During the past generation, and especially during the past two decades, once discrete and separate tools, machines, and processes increasingly have been fitting together into what is now a continuous-production machine-complex. Devices which once stood apart have been modified and shoved together back-to-back or arranged side-by-side. Then the material moves without interruption through a series of production stages, and the job of the men is to co-ordinate the component devices rather than to work on the material itself.

This stage of almost automatic production is a kind of primitive automation, a Neanderthal version of the automatic factory. Mere mortals, however, have trouble operating and regulating these massive, complicatedly interrelated conglomerations of machinery. Some self-regulation can be built into such equipment, as in the printing press, but the continuously co-ordinated activity of dozens or even scores of individual devices depends upon the operators to read the right instruments at the right times and to respond quickly enough with the proper turning of dials and punching of buttons.

Even though control of such a line is divided up among several men, with a top operator in charge of the over-all functioning, they can watch only a relatively few meters, lights, and other instruments in order to find out what may be going on from one moment to the next in every hidden and visible part of the mechanical monster. Because of this limitation, production bangs to an emergency stop at least several times on almost every shift. Given human operation of the line, quality control is often difficult, and many kinds of production simply cannot be reduced to an uninterrupted flow of materials and activity "untouched by human hands."

The Electronic Computer

It is this problem which is solved by automation. The electronic computer takes over most of the task of control once handled or mishandled by human operatives. Properly set up ("programmed")—and this is a fantastically complicated undertaking—all parts of the machine-complex continuously send information to the computer through the various control circuits. It evaluates this information and on the basis of the evaluation selects the appropriate alterations in the settings of the various controls in order to maintain uninterrupted and nearly flawless production. Practically speaking, the computer continuously adjusts and readjusts all the component parts of the line. If there is some unavoidable breakdown, it informs the operators and maintenance men where the trouble is and pretty much what it is.

The computer, of course, does not "think." The kinds of evaluations it can make and the alternative adjustments it can call for are predetermined by the programming. But it can be "loaded" with enough information and ways of handling it to make an unanticipated contingency requiring initiative and imagination most unlikely. Professor Richard L. Meier pointed out not long ago that the programming is so difficult and sophisticated a task that lack of trained personnel counts, along with cost of investment, as a major brake on the trend toward automation.

New Kind of Worker Required by Automation

Just as automation requires a new kind of engineer, it also demands a new kind of worker. It is not that now there must be electronics technicians in addition to electricians. The workers, especially those on production jobs, must learn to be preoccupied by the relationships of machines to one another, while the machinery works on the material from which, in a psychological sense, the operative is now insulated.

Even the man who manages to move from an old-style job to a new one may hang on only at the cost of much irritation and frustration. "Old Stash," for example, is an operative on a part of one of the semiautomatic devices to which true automation has not yet been applied; but he cannot really understand even this machine-complex. For years before the line for the continuous production of tin-plate by electrolysis was introduced, Stash had stood at one end of an old hot-dip stack and shoved steel plate, one sheet at a time, into a little system of rollers and belts which carried it through a preparing process and a tank of molten tin and out again. He could comprehend what it did.

Now he is part of a team of men who work in co-operation with the vast electronic control system which secretly and silently goes about its mysterious activity in the basement beneath the floor on which he stands. While the men signal to each other with lights and bells, the steel flashes by at seven or eight hundred feet per minute, emerging as tinplate cut to size, stacked on skids ready to be wrapped for shipping. Stash knows he will never be an operator. It is not that he cannot read the schematics of the control system. Perhaps more important, he just cannot think in the way the new technology requires. He still has his mind on the hardness of the material instead of the complexity of the relationships.

One consequence of automation, then, could be a reinforcing of the pattern of old age as a time of decline in the work-career of the industrial laborer, a kind of "aging" which might begin long before the time of retirement was reached. As Dr. Gordon S. Brown of the Massachusetts Institute of Technology has pointed out, while automation will create many new upgraded jobs, it is often the young man from trade school or college who moves into the new position instead of the older worker whose skill has suddenly become obsolete.[1] "This makes it a young man's game," Dr. Brown observed, "but we can't overlook the fact that the oldsters still have to play."

[1] Gordon S. Brown, "Automation," a statement before the Fiftieth Anniversary Conference of the League for Industrial Democracy, New York, April 22, 1955.

On-the-Job Training

To enable the old-timer to play the production game in an age of automation, Dr. Brown urged that management undertake extensive on-the-job training in advance of the introduction of computer-controlled equipment. He urged unions to encourage job mobility and versatility, to seek the upgraded job rather than engage in a fruitless rearguard defense of the old, and to re-examine in this light the vested pension, the rigid job classification, or the seniority program.

Today, on-the-job training in most factories is meager, if it exists at all. Traditionally, in most industries the worker is given a "fair shake" at a new position, a formal or informal probationary period during which he must master the new skills by doing the work. Usually, he has had some experience on the job previously, perhaps as a relief man or a replacement for someone who was sick. Unless he is unusually disliked, those who already know the work will help him. Most on-the-job training programs have only extended, formalized, and supplemented this traditional system. They tend to be brief and to deal almost entirely with operational matters pertinent to the particular function the promoted or about-to-be promoted employee expects to assume. They presuppose that the new job calls only for particular new techniques or skills and not for whole new attitudes toward work, whole new conceptions of machinery and of processes of production.

How do you train people to incorporate fundamentally changed notions of work and of their images of themselves as producers? How long should it take? As the traditional system suggests, workers tend to think in concrete terms

about particulars rather than in the abstract about gener-
alities. How can they be trained to think in a way commensurate with the demands of automation before they
have had a chance to live with it for a while; and, on the
other hand, what would be the consequences of letting
them live with it before they had been retrained, so that
training could genuinely be "on-the-job"? Asking old-
timers to "go to school" for training, which young men
just hiring in already have, also has some difficult status
implications. Can these be mitigated?

None of these questions detracts from the basic merits
of Dr. Brown's approach to the problems of the older
worker in the forthcoming age of automation. Those who
prefer this approach to some others must be prepared to
cope with the realities of the industrial life of our society.

Retraining Programs

Most industrial managers cannot be expected to be enthusiastic supporters of proposals for extensive retraining
programs. At least where the hourly paid employees are
concerned, supervisors are inclined to believe that old
dogs cannot be taught new tricks, especially if the new
trick is quite different from any that has previously been
mastered. Managers fear not only that outmoded preconceptions will not be unlearned and replaced, but also that
the old-timers may bring with them long-standing union-
management tensions which the company prefers to keep
out of the new department. In one instance, men were
taken for a radically new production line with the understanding that they would be paid their previous "average
earnings" during the break-in period for learning the operations. But they also had to "come in through the gate"—
to hire in as new employees at the expense of whatever
seniority they had accumulated. This, of course, was a

high price for the "old dogs" to pay for learning even a whole set of new tricks.

This same attitude toward the older workers sometimes leads to efforts to shift them from jobs being changed by the oncoming technological revolution to the remaining old-style activities that are of as nearly commensurate skill and pay level as is possible. Then the younger men are brought in as pioneers. This, however, is a technique limited by available openings and by a system of seniority (often including departmental rights) to which the workers are for good reasons deeply committed.

It seems to me that there is a more fundamental problem here. Professor David Riesman has cautioned that many proposals to aid the aging often can become additions to those patterns of later life in our society which sustain and protect the older person at the cost of confining him and of denying to him the chance to develop intellectual and spiritual aspects of his personality to compensate for—and perhaps indirectly to inhibit—physical decay. The older person is denied the chance to maintain the psychological anabolism involved in meeting challenges in the face of the physical catabolism which is inevitable with the passing of the years.[2] Riesman points to such extreme and therefore clear and useful examples of men who, in a sense, go on "growing" instead of "aging," such as Bertrand Russell and Toscanini. Certainly lesser men can avoid stagnation or retrogression in less spectacular ways.

Ability of Older Workers to Surmount Changes

The image of the old age of the industrial worker as a negative climax to accumulated weariness distorted as

[2] David Riesman, "Some Clinical and Cultural Aspects of Aging," *Amer. Journ. Sociol.*, 19 (1954): 379–83.

well as reflected the reality from which it developed. Not all millhands during the first two centuries of factory industrialism were brutalized by their labor each day or left prematurely aged by it to eke out some miserable existence until death sent them to that happy factory in the skies. Highly skilled mechanics accustomed to the extended hours and heavy labor of their times enjoyed life both in and outside of the factory. It is true that many of them worked until they dropped, but many also did not drop for a long, long time. Such old-time machinists and mechanics seem to personify the potential vitality of many older workers, for they have adjusted to and sometimes helped bring about many technological changes. In many instances management has turned to them because they have kept abreast of new developments and have the practical know-how to help take the "bugs" out of the new machinery. Younger men, preoccupied by life concerns outside the mill and with trying to learn all that the older worker already knows, may be less prepared for the change.

Historically, other workers have surmounted the huge obstacles to making life outside the mill more than a dismal cycle. "Do-it-yourself" has long been a part of American working class culture. Frederick Taylor, describing his pioneer experiments with time study and other devices of "scientific management," tells how, about the time of the Spanish-American War, he made use of a Dutch immigrant who trotted home after loading pig iron by hand each day and worked on a little house he was building for himself. It seems clear from Taylor's description that this man (although Taylor thought him extremely dull) was in fact one of those individuals who enjoy challenges. He agreed on the basis of very little advance information to participate in the time-and-motion study experiment and apparently easily accepted the great alteration in work procedures which came with it.

A little talk on automation was delivered to a regional institute for local union officers and rank and file members by the recording secretary of a local union, an experienced, old-time mechanic. He tangled with mixed success with the phraseology of the new technology—cybernetics, servomechanisms, feedback and the like; but it was clear that he thoroughly understood the basic principles of the new industrial techniques. Of course, machinists and mechanics who learn to handle each new piece of equipment as it comes into the shop have some advantage over those production workers who may become entrenched in one kind of productive process over the years.

Nevertheless, the advent of automation could for many older workers be a saving challenge instead of the final guarantee of their obsolescence. Much depends upon whether or not either the workers or the managers are convinced that old dogs do not learn new tricks. There is a subtle but fundamental difference between presenting the possibility of trying out on the new equipment as "a chance" instead of "the last chance." The worker who gave the talk on automation to his fellow union members said that he viewed this as the opening of a "golden age," bringing with it even shorter hours and easier work than has already been achieved.

Such a viewpoint, focusing upon life inside the factory, is quite different from that which sees automation hastening the decline of older workers and their exodus from the plant into the limbo or promised land of retirement. The mill of the future very well could be a place where men worked without loss of status or ability until they were far older than has been true at any time in the past. It is therefore necessary to speculate about the relative appeals of retirement, on the one hand, and of continued work, on the other, as automation alters the nature of the industrial experience.

Effects of Retirement

Among the millworkers there are two versions of the legend that factory laborers die shortly after they quit working. One version has it that the job is the keystone of life, and when it falls out the rest crumbles. The second and now most popular version asserts that all the life has been worked out of a man by the time he is old enough to have to quit or to be retired. The conclusion following from this second version is that the age of retirement ought to be drastically reduced.

In conversations about retirement with three different millhands in the same department—one who is twenty-six, one who is thirty-four, and one who is fifty-four—their remarks, typical of industrial workers, were practically interchangeable in spite of their different ages and backgrounds: "No man should have to spend his life working in the mill," they said. Retirement should begin at fifty-five as a maximum, or at fifty if possible. Even forty-five did not seem too young. The rest of life could then be used to do all those things for which one never had time and energy enough while putting in eight hours a day five or six days a week at the plant.

The men vowed they would not find time hanging heavy on their hands once they lacked a job. There was so much to do in life besides work in a factory! At last a man could finish his home and landscape his yard, and even be able to "piddle" at it instead of having to drive himself to get done all that he could on a one- or two-day weekend. And then maybe he could build a house for one of his kids. Since millworkers often do much or all of their own labor, building a house can involve a year of nearly full-time work rather than the five minutes necessary to sign a contract and write a check.

At last a man would have time to hunt and fish—not the little bits and moments of these ancient, traditional past times which weekends and vacations now afford, but those long stretches for which every true fisherman and hunter always yearn. There would be travel. The workers, with some exceptions, have a lust for travel that seems to exceed almost every other single desire. Since they demand only a trailer, or an inexpensive motel, or a tent for lodging, their budgets for travel are far below those which most middle class people require. Many workers who retire at fifty-five, anticipating an active life for twenty more years, could reasonably expect to spend at least a third and perhaps half of that time traveling—to see the sights and to visit distant relatives and friends.

Some industrial laborers already have started small enterprises to which they expect to devote themselves when they retire—farms, lunch counters, motels, service stations, corner groceries. They use their mill incomes to launch and keep going these ventures until they retire, and then with their retirement incomes can afford to continue the enterprises even if they are not very profitable, just so long as this is what they want to do. The next two decades probably will see the poultry business confronted by a host of small-scale operators who will stay in the market even if they lose a little just because all their lives they wanted to raise chickens. Another version of this came from a long-active union officer and his wife who told me that, once retired, they expect to hold down some of the important but low-paying union and political jobs which ordinarily go begging or are filled by incompetents because they do not provide an adequate income.

It may be that we are witnessing the conjunction of two very important trends—the first, automation, making the latter years of industrial work life even more likely to be a time of possibly precipitous decline in job status; the second, the improving provisions and increasingly intense desire for retirement, lessening the older inclination to "hang on" somehow. If this is the case, the next two decades will see strong campaigns for the rapid lowering of retirement age in both government and union-management programs, as well as for substantial increases in benefits. We will find the older workers, like our teen-agers, becoming a major bloc of consumers of the products and services of industries that provide for leisure and recreation. And we can expect them, like the teen-agers, to influence the patterns of leisure and recreation enjoyed by those of us in the age grades that cannot so fully follow these pursuits.

Certainly the problems of aging for industrial workers in general are different from those faced by older people who are at least partially isolated from the mainstreams of our culture in forlorn flats in the city or little shacks in the country, or even in those sometimes plush preserves set aside in warmer climes. Most of the workers clearly intend to remain active and effective members of kinship groups, of extended and quasi-families, of various cliques, associations and organizations—all cutting across the generational lines and age grades. As much as I am concerned about what we do to and for them, I am equally concerned about what they will do to and for us. How they behave will certainly reflect back upon the younger groups as a model for what the yet-to-be aged hope to attain or avoid when *they* become old-timers. Since we all live consciously and unconsciously in anticipation of the future as well as in reaction to the past, what has consequence for the culture of the old-timers cannot help but affect the whole fabric of our lives.

In this sense we ought to engage in some especially hypothetical speculation about the impact automation may have upon the *next* generation of aging factory workers. We can anticipate some of their characteristics. They will be adjusted to the new modes of production and will not be likely to face the kind of skill obsolescence which has confronted so many millhands today and in times past. Like the machinist and the mechanic, they will be flexible in their thinking and adaptable in their techniques. In addition, the work will be of such a nature that physical weakening, until it becomes quite extensive, will have little effect on the job performance; while the experience and accumulated know-how that comes from working with automated equipment will be highly prized.

Let us add to this a number of suppositions, all of which are definitely possibilities, whatever the probability: suppose that the older workers now anticipating retirement with such glee find, as they live longer and retire earlier, that some aspects of life they strongly desire are lacking— the power over things which is so much a part of their self-image and which they derive largely from millwork, the camaraderie of the shop and of the essentially all-male society in the factory, and simply those comforting aspects of established routine which they now overlook because of a preoccupying distaste for monotony. Suppose also that much shorter hours and much longer vacations enable the workers to enjoy many of those life activities which today seem possible only as alternatives to full-time work.

While automation is likely in the near future to intensify the drive for earlier and better-supported retirement, in the more distant future and in combination with other trends it might well facilitate a reversal and a rejection of

early retirement. Since automation will diminish somewhat our industrial manpower needs, and since old-timers
often tend to hold substantial power in both unions and
politics, this might result in a shift from retirement to take
willing aging workers out of the labor market to more education plus military or CCC-type service for the young in
order to delay their entrance into the labor market.

It should be clear in considering the consequences of
automation for the older workers and other age levels,
that technological change of this sort does not have any
single predetermined outcome. Sometimes, with a kind of
subtle animism, we seem to imbue technology with the
characteristics of fate: this-or-that invention changed the
course of human history in this-or-that particular way. Our
concern with automation should demonstrate to us that
technology is but one of a number of interacting variables
each of which at one time or another may have greater or
lesser influence than the rest. What we are really asking,
it seems to me, is not "What will automation do to us?"
but, rather, "Given automation, what are we going to do
to ourselves and to each other?"

The walls are not yet made of marble, except in the
front offices and the latrines of some of the newest factories. The machines, in spite of an increasing content of
precious metals, are still made of well-greased steel instead of gleaming gold. Workers continue to move along
inevitably toward "later maturity," but automation is
hurrying us into an era in which the industrial laborer in
fact will never get tired (at least physically) because of his
job activity. We will probably deal with this and with the
other implications of automation for older workers in a
variety of ways, at least for quite a while; and I suspect
this is best however much it may add to our practical and

theoretical problems. We are a diverse nation and automation clearly is not one, but a bundle of problems. We need every bit of imagination and experimentation we can manage: earlier retirement and longer job careers, retraining programs and replacement programs, ever-higher status for older workers and a new dominance for young men. Each will make its appearance somewhere and it is up to us to observe and evaluate as best we can the virtues and vices of each reaction.

2. For the Employment of the Aging

JAMES STERN

James Stern, Ph.D., is staff consultant for the UAW-CIO Automation Committee. He has been a representative of the UAW-CIO since 1946, serving first as the assistant director of the Research and Engineering Department in charge of engineering, and later as a labor designee to the Economic Cooperation Administration in Paris.

What is Automation?

AUTOMATION is more than invention. It is the widespread acceptance and usage of the basic principles of automatic operation and control. When applied to the startling advances in basic human knowledge, automation transforms industrial and commercial life. Traditional concepts and familiar scenes are disappearing. Production must be redesigned. Factory size and location will be changed. Compartmentalized engineering as it exists today is obsolete. From the raw material to the finished product of the office and factory, automation replaces the tried and true with new and amazing techniques.

Many scientists state that there are three main subdivisions of automation. One, Detroit automation, consists of the grouping of many standard tools on one large base. The part to be processed is automatically loaded, machined, and unloaded. The operator is not directly involved in the production process. This gigantic machine is controlled by means of an electric panel board with many flashing lights. Only when these lights indicate that some trouble has arisen does an operator investigate and correct the trouble. *Business Week* described one example of Detroit automation used in the machining of jet engines: "Using 55 carbide tools at about 600 H.P., this many-armed monster does at one clip for 90 cents what used to cost $1200. . . . It condenses a 20 acre plant into 20 square feet. It costs $500,000—but replaces $52 million worth of machines." [1]

A second kind of automation is described as feedback automation. Technically, feedback can be described as a system in which the output is compared with the desired value, with the difference being used to activate a controller or servomechanism (that is, a small motor) to make the appropriate correction. It is a self-regulating system in which any deviation from a standard automatically activates a correcting counteractivity until finally the exact predetermined standard is achieved.

The thermostat in our homes is a simple example of feedback. One sets the dial at 68°. If the room temperature is under 68°, the furnace automatically goes into operation, heats the room, and then when it reaches the required temperature, is turned off automatically. Later on, when the room cools off, the thermostat again signals the furnace to supply heat. When the family goes out to the neighborhood movie, everyone assumes that the thermostat will continue to work even though no one is around to observe it. But when this same principle is applied to regulate a large, modern refinery, it tends to overawe us. There a dozen men sitting in a control room operate a modern petroleum refinery covering many acres of ground.

A third kind of automation could be called computer automation. Computers were popularized over night when millions of people saw Univac predict the results of our elections. The same kind of computer is being used by the General Electric Company and others to make out pay-

[1] *Business Week,* Sept. 4, 1954, p. 88.

rolls and to handle routine inventory, filing, and billing automatically. At the Massachusetts Institute of Technology, a computer is used to translate instructions from a paper tape into the appropriate commands for an automatic milling machine. This milling machine, operating at the command of the computer, can turn out any piece that a skilled machinist can make. It performs faster and with fewer mistakes than does a human being.

It is clear to workers in offices and factories throughout the country that radical changes are taking place. Wartime developments, such as atomic energy, guided missiles, automatic gun tracking and gun firing devices, have been converted to peacetime uses. The principles behind these wartime inventions are used in the automatic control devices running factories and offices. Group research in university and corporation laboratories has accelerated the flow of new techniques and machines. Modern communication has shortened the lag between invention and application. A laboratory discovery of today is applied in the factory in a remarkably short time. Automation, however, is much more than a speeding up of the old kind of technological change. Large quantitative changes are accompanied now by significant qualitative changes.

In the past, machine power replaced human muscle power. Today, mechanical judgment replaces human judgment. We have built machines that see, hear, and feel. We have constructed machines that profit by experience. These machines have memory units and in effect can be said to learn. Machines inspect, then reject or accept the products they are turning out; in many cases they even correct their own errors.

For perhaps the first time in the history of man, we have reached the stage where our scientific prowess has provided the tools for the abolition of poverty and scarcity. These tools, however, must be used intelligently or a great opportunity for human advancement will be missed. Even worse, these tools can be applied in a socially irresponsible fashion, to cause widespread disruption and untold hardships for millions of workers.

The challenge of automation is clear. Can we match our scientific progress with comprehensive, carefully thought-out social policies? The undesirable by-products of rapid change must be kept at a minimum. The wealth made available by automation must be distributed wisely and used fairly for the benefit of all.

Automation and Full Employment

The major problem to be faced is the maintenance of full employment within the context of an expanding economy. The rapid acceleration of productivity associated with automation requires that greater attention be given to this task. When the number of job seekers exceeds the number of job opportunities, women, Negroes, unskilled workers, and workers over forty-five find it particularly difficult to gain employment. Given the present social climate, older workers and the other disadvantaged groups bear the burden of our failure to utilize automation wisely.

In the past, our economy has expended its output at an average annual rate of approximately 2½ to 3 per cent. Today, automation has given rise to a situation in which productivity appears to be increasing at approximately twice the historic rate. For example, productivity in industry increased more than 5 per cent between November 1953 and November 1954.

No one objects to increased productivity, but increased

productivity without increased over-all production is a clear-cut formula for depression. Total industrial output was exactly the same in November 1954 as in November 1953. The 5 per cent increase in productivity meant that approximately one million of the 17 million industrial employees lost their jobs during that year.[2] The same volume of goods was turned out by fewer workers, while at the same time the number of job seekers increased by 1 per cent because of normal population growth.

These developments explain the increase in unemployment during this period from a low of 1.5 million to over 3 million. And, as was pointed out in the Haber study[3] a few years ago, older workers on the average are unemployed longer than young workers and a disproportionate number of older workers are among those unemployed long enough to exhaust their claim to benefits.

Therefore, to the extent that we have not expanded total output commensurate with the productivity gains of automation, automation will heighten the insecurity of all workers, but in particular will have an adverse effect on the lives of older workers and other disadvantaged groups.

The Industrial Structure of Our Economy

Automation gives rise to the forced draft obsolescence of our industrial structure and accelerates the replacement of plant and equipment by new, different, dispersed, and decentralized facilities. The enormous increase in potential

[2] The Federal Reserve Board Index of industrial production was 132 per cent in November 1953 and November 1954 (not adjusted seasonally). Dept. of Commerce and Dept. of Labor releases showed industrial employment down during this period from 16,988,000 to 16,107,000.

[3] William Haber, "How Much Does It Cost?" A report to the Michigan Employment Security Commission on long-range unemployment insurance benefit financing and fund solvency in Michigan, Spring, 1951.

output per plant, based on increased output per unit of floor space, has significant consequences.

Major companies find that they need no longer rely on suppliers. Automation increases the tendency toward vertical integration. The cost of an automated plant is high. It is in the interest of a plant management to reduce production cost by running this plant at capacity throughout the year. If sales of the product are not increased sufficiently, the automated plant can be utilized more fully by the making of parts formerly purchased from small supplier plants.

Automation gives rise also to horizontal integration. The increased potential capacity of each plant and corporation lessens the number of companies that will be able to compete successfully with each other. The cost of automation equipment is high; extensive research and planning precede its adoption. These characteristics give the giant corporation an enormous advantage over its smaller competitor. For the smaller plant to survive, it frequently must merge with others. The creation in the auto industry of the "little three," Kaiser-Willys, Studebaker-Packard, and Hudson-Nash, illustrates this consequence of automation. Not only is the number of mergers on the increase, but we are also witnessing the gobbling up of small firms by larger ones in the new fields of the making of automation equipment. General Electric and IBM have purchased new, promising, small electronic equipment concerns. In some cases, a famous producer in one field, with ample financial backing, is entrenching itself in a new and completely unrelated field. General Mills, heretofore thought of as the father of Jack Armstrong and the maker of Wheaties, is an important supplier of automatic equipment for the manufacture of radios, TV sets, computers, and military electronic equipment. Their famous masterpiece, "Autofab," an automatic assembly machine, is displacing hundreds of workers who formerly assembled radio and TV sets by hand.

The elimination of supplier firms, the many mergers (with the attendant closing down of the older facilities of the merged firms), and the expansion of old, established firms into new and unrelated fields have a significant effect on older workers. Automation does not alter the fact that it usually takes an older worker longer to find a new job than a young worker, assuming all other factors are equal. Automation does mean, however, that the older worker faces this situation more frequently than in the past. His disadvantage is greater for reasons to be discussed later, and he faces this disadvantage more often. For example, the Murray Body Corporation formerly supplied the Ford Motor Company with some of the fenders, hoods, roofs, and floors for Ford automobiles. Ford expanded and automated its stamping plants to provide sufficient capacity to handle all of its needs itself, and cancelled the supplier contract with Murray Body.

Murray Body, seeing the handwriting on the wall, protected the interests of its management and stockholders by making an agreement with Brunswick-Collender, a major bowling ball manufacturer, to supply it with automatic pin-setting equipment. This equipment, which may be seen at bowling alleys around the country, is not made in the old Murray Body plant in Detroit but in a newer plant in New Jersey. The Detroit plant is down, the buildings and machinery are for sale, and the five thousand employees at this plant started looking for jobs last summer. Interviews with some of these workers revealed that the younger workers gained employment far more easily than the old. Racial and sexual discrimination appear to be less important in this instance than discrimination on the basis of age. An over-all statistical study of the Murray employees is under way at present. I suspect it will strengthen rather than weaken the evidence derived from the interviews.

One woman, forty-nine, with twenty-five years' seniority at Murray Body as a small press operator and seamstress on auto trim, looked for work, found none, exhausted her unemployment compensation, and now spends her time around the home. She is no longer even listed as unemployed. Automation in her case meant her involuntary retirement from the Detroit labor force at a time when younger women were being hired in automobile plants.

Two Negroes, one thirty-three and one fifty-five, attempted to find jobs at the same shops. The thirty-three-year-old found work at a Chrysler plant after six months of job hunting, was again laid off and found another job at a different Chrysler plant within a week. The fifty-five-year-old, however, stated he had been told, "We're not hiring," at both of these plants at the same time his thirty-three-year-old friend was hired. The fifty-five-year-old finally got a job the other day after eleven months of unemployment. He is a sweeper at fifteen cents an hour less than he used to receive at Murray as a packer-crater. He is on the night shift, whereas formerly he was on the day shift. He lost his pension rights and other benefits. His twelve years of Murray Body seniority are gone—he is a probationary employee at the new plant.

A fifty-two-year-old die setter and a sixty-two-year-old millwright told stories similar to the above, except that neither of them had yet found jobs when they were interviewed two months ago.

The rapidly changing industrial structure accompanying the installation of automation appears to throw an unfair burden on the shoulders of older workers. They are forced to change jobs more frequently now in a social setting that penalizes them arbitrarily for their age.

Job Content

In some respects, however, automation changes job content in a manner which actually makes the older worker a more desirable job candidate than a young worker. Characteristically, an automated job is one on which all or almost all physical effort has been eliminated or greatly reduced. Manual loading, transferring, and unloading are eliminated. The operator is a machine attendant, or watchman, or caretaker. His responsibility is greatly increased as the amount of machinery under his control is much larger than formerly.

Traditionally, caretaker and watchman jobs have been allotted to older workers because of the light physical demands of these occupations. More and more the average factory job will be that of machine attendant and button pusher, jobs with equally light physical demands. Employer statements to the effect that the physical effort requirements on these jobs bar the use of older workers would appear to be hypocritical.

The decreased physical effort and increased responsibility on most automated jobs make the mature, responsible, reliable worker a better choice in many instances than the husky adolescent. In one new automated plant where the typical discriminatory policies were followed, the average age of the work force was approximately twenty-five. During the course of a labor dispute at this plant, the plant manager admitted ruefully that the policy of hiring only the young had its drawbacks. He has a volatile work force and, as he pointed out, he now sees that he would have been much better off if he had hired some older men with families, homes, and a more responsible outlook on life.

If his changed views were echoed by others, it would greatly improve the chances of employment for older workers.

Training and Retraining

Many experts believe that automation will bring about another change in our labor force—a more rapid upgrading of skills and occupations. A prominent management spokesman described this effect of automation in the following words: "The hand trucker of today replaced by a conveyor belt might become tomorrow's electronics engineer. . . . Drill press operators replaced by automatic multiple drilling machines could be trained as future tool makers." [4]

I assume that there is agreement in principle with the desire underlying this statement. A hand trucker might become an electronics engineer; a drill press operator could be trained as a tool maker. All of us hope that the worker between forty-five and sixty-five whose job is eliminated can find another job. And, if his skill is made obsolete by automation, we hope he will be able to acquire training which will provide him with a new skill. The facts of life are such, however, that the quotation above tends to remain a pious declaration of what should and could be, rather than what is and well may be.

Our older workers on the average have less formal education than younger workers. Those who specialize in older workers' problems know the degree of truth in the widely accepted statement that it is easier to train new workers than to retrain older workers. How flexible are older workers? Will they want to and will they be able to train for new and different occupations? Tool makers and

[4] R. H. Sullivan, Vice President and Group Executive, Ford Motor Company, quoted in *Wall Street Journal*, Dec. 31, 1953.

electronics engineers are not trained over night—under present arrangements lengthy training courses are required. How will the income of the older worker be maintained while he is in training? If the new job is in a different community, where will he get the money to relocate his family? There are many difficult questions to be solved and they will not be solved until we face up to the basic economics involved. All of us have a responsibility to that generation of workers made obsolete by the application of our new knowledge. In our rapid strides to new plateaus in living, I am confident that we do not wish to be haunted by the ghosts of the generation of forgotten men.

We will have these ghosts in our closets, however, unless we examine and reduce the divergence between the private cost and the social cost of upgrading our labor force. Under present-day circumstances, individual managements first try to find already trained young men for the new jobs. These workers are trained at community expense under our philosophy of free public education. In some cases this has paid a part of the cost of their advanced training. As long as these men are available to an employer he finds it cheaper to hire them than to retrain older workers. He keeps his private costs, the expenditures on his books, to a minimum. When the community allows a forty-five-year-old man to be turned out without retraining, however, we suffer a social cost. We lose the productive service of this man while he is unemployed, not to mention the cost of unemployment benefits. If he is re-employed finally in an unskilled job after failing to find work at his old trade, we are forcing a downgrading. We are not allowing this man to participate to the utmost limit of his latent potential.

All of us pay this social cost. Individual managements, however, carry a private cost which in no sense reflects a full share of the social cost. If we are to do something about the problem of retraining the older worker we must reduce the divergence between private and social cost. If it remains more profitable for management to avoid its responsibilities for retraining, it will in most cases do so. If the economics of the retraining situation are such that, costwise, retraining an older worker is the same as hiring an already trained young worker, one of the biggest barriers to the retraining of older workers will have been removed.

This gap between private and social cost is, in my opinion, the basis for the widespread prejudice against hiring older workers. Take away the money incentive to discriminate and you take away much of the discrimination. Take away the money incentive to discriminate and then the training problems of older workers can be attacked vigorously with a good chance of success.

Leisure

In addition to the vocational training for older workers that automation makes more pressing, our entire educational system must be reoriented. In ten years, a continuation of the increased productivity associated with automation will make possible, for example, a four-day week, a 20 per cent increase in per capita income, and a change in our labor force participation rates. It will permit older people who wish to do so to retire earlier on adequate pensions, and allow younger people to stay in school longer to receive the training required in our society of tomorrow. It is true that we could take all of the increased wealth we generate through automation in the form of goods and services and thereby almost double our standard of living. Historically, however, we have chosen increased leisure along with a higher standard of living.

Youngsters in grammar school today will probably grow up accustomed to the four-day week and will wonder at our work schedules, just as we wonder at our fathers' and grandfathers'. But what about *our* attitudes toward leisure and the attitudes of workers over forty-five? The sociologists delight in telling us ours is a work-oriented and highly materialistic culture. If this is true, basic cultural changes must accompany automation.

Recreational, cultural, and educational facilities are already overcrowded. An increase in leisure time would require an immediate large scale expansion of these facilities. Pensions must be increased also or retirement will not truly provide leisure. Leisure time without the economic resources, adequate physical facilities, and a positive social orientation will be meaningless. If these problems are not solved, society will be faced with the dilemma that Robert Hutchins posed for America in a recent speech in which he said that "Americans can either blow themselves to bits with thermonuclear weapons or bore themselves to death with the leisure time that automation provides." There is a third choice, however, a satisfactory life based upon a successful use of leisure time as well as job opportunities for all at the upper limits of individual competence.

The UAW-CIO Program

The problems associated with the harnessing of automation are big, and big problems demand big solutions. Each must do his part. Speaking as a member and representative of one of the large unions in the UAW-CIO, I want to say that we in the UAW will do our best to live up to our responsibilities. We are demanding and negotiating a guaranteed annual wage that will alleviate hardship during the forced shift from job to job. After the guaranteed annual wage has been won, the demand for a shorter work-week will be placed at the top of the UAW collective bargaining agenda.

We recognize also that purchasing power must be increased greatly to keep it in balance with our expanded productive power. The annual improvement factor clause in our contracts gives recognition to this principle. We have increased the size of the annual improvement factor from three cents per hour to four, to five, and now to six cents an hour or 2½ per cent of the hourly wage (whichever is the greater). We are demanding short term contracts so that we will have the flexibility to make the adjustments necessitated by automation.

Local unions all over the country are meeting with their representative managements in attempts to modernize the wage, classification, and seniority systems in the plants under UAW contract. In effect, we are saying that where management has automated production we will automate the wage, classification, and seniority structure.

This portion of the UAW program is particularly important to the older worker. For the most part he is a high seniority worker. In those plants where seniority is on a departmental basis, the installation of one machine may wipe out his years of seniority and eliminate his job. At the same time a younger worker with less than a year's seniority will continue to work in a department across the aisle from the older worker's former work place.

Departmental seniority is obsolete. Automation makes necessary the widest possible seniority base if we are to keep to a minimum and share equitably the disruption accompanying automation. In the plants of the major con-

cerns, corporation-wide seniority will protect older workers replaced by new facilities. Older workers in smaller
firms can be protected by the negotiation of preferential
hiring rights in the same industry and area. In addition,
severance pay, retraining pay, and relocation allowances
will enable the older worker to cope with the problems of
an industry in transformation far better than he can at
present.

UAW's Position Regarding Automation

I should make clear that the UAW has frequently and
publicly stated its position as regards automation. We do
not oppose automation. We favor the introduction of the
much more efficient work methods associated with automation. We see in these developments a remarkable
chance to increase living standards. We believe, furthermore, that automation provides such great wealth that it
would be socially irresponsible and morally unforgivable
if some of this new abundance that automation makes
possible is not devoted to the smoothing of the transition
for the workers directly affected. Some groups in our country say that the UAW opposes automation. They cite our
efforts to minimize the disruption that may accompany the
widespread installation of automation. To them I would
say that any intelligent person should be concerned with
the socially undesirable by-products of rapid change. To
label as anti-progressive those in society who voice a
legitimate concern with these by-products is in actuality
an effort to shut one's eyes to the problems that historically have accompanied rapid strides to new and higher
plateaus of human satisfaction and economic well being.

Some of you may question whether the UAW is successful in implementing its program to harness automation in
a socially responsible fashion. A straightforward answer is

that we have begun to make progress but still have a long way to go.

It is not easy to convince management, in many instances, of the necessity of automating the wage, classification, and seniority structures. But in some plants we have successfully negotiated new classifications such as "automation tender" to cover the men on automated equipment. We have broadened seniority within plants and among plants of the same corporation. We have insisted successfully, in some instances, that seniority be the governing factor in bidding on jobs in new automated plants located adjacent to existing facilities. In the area of retraining, however, we have made little progress. We face a strong resistance from the managements with which we bargain. Management speaks often of the need for men with the new skills required by automation but, because of the cost factor mentioned previously, has to date resisted the establishment of adequate retraining programs.

We should not underestimate the problems of automation. Unions and managements, across the bargaining table, can solve only some of them. All of us have a responsibility—government, citizens, and experts on the problems of the aging. The government, for example, will have a major responsibility for the expansion of the school system, the handling of the problem of increasing economic concentration, the maintenance of full employment, the expansion of public facilities for retraining, education, and recreation.

From the standpoint of those interested in helping the older workers, the challenges are many. Can you devise short term retraining programs within the capacities of the older worker that will make him a desirable employee in an automated plant? Can you show clearly the extent to which older workers are discriminated against and how this discrimination can be eliminated? Can you make suggestions that will facilitate the enjoyment of leisure by citizens brought up to work and unprepared for greater leisure time?

Automation offers all of us the opportunity to move speedily to the point where economic needs will be fulfilled to a far greater extent than ever before. We will have an unheard of opportunity to develop our spiritual, social, and educational desires. For future generations these problems may be slight and their chances for a satisfactory life may be favorable. But, for the older worker, there are many immediate and large problems which must be solved.

Some people, however, tend to focus their attention on noncontroversial problems such as the expansion of the "do-it-yourself" activities for the aged. If we are really to help the older worker we must do much more than this. We can help other groups working on these problems by outlining the types of programs that will be needed to enable our older workers to fulfill a useful and needed role in society.

Automation will not be a hindrance. With it we will have the wealth to finance whatever programs are necessary. With it comes a greater stress on maturity, responsibility, training, and skill. Physical effort requirements, the age-old enemy of the older worker, are now almost eliminated. The future of the older worker can be bright if we recognize our opportunity to accelerate our application of social "know why" to match the unprecedented application of our technical "know how."

A MODERN PATTERN
FOR MEETING
THE HEALTH NEEDS
OF THE AGING *Chapter III*

HERMAN E. HILLEBOE, M.D.

> *Herman E. Hilleboe, M.D., is commissioner of health
> of the New York State Department of Health. Before
> assuming this position in 1947 he was professor of
> public health and preventive medicine at Albany
> Medical School, and associate professor of public
> health at Columbia University School of Public
> Health. He is a member of a panel of tuberculosis
> experts of the World Health Organization and is the
> author of* Essentials of Pulmonary Tuberculosis.

OUR POPULATION is growing older as our life span is extended by public health service and medical care. Vital
statistics show that in 1975 the number of people over
sixty-five in New York state will be double that of 1955.

A health program for older people cannot start at age
sixty, or sixty-five, or seventy; it must begin during adult
life at the time when chronic diseases begin to attack the
aging body. A sound program directed against the chronic
diseases of adult life—heart disease, cancer, diabetes, arthritis—is truly preventive geriatrics. As the work capacity
and reserve strength begin to dwindle in middle age and
later years, health resources must be measured. Individuals vary greatly in their rate of physiological aging. These
rates of aging vary also with sex, race, and social and eco-

nomic status. Housing conditions and occupational opportunities are important factors that affect the health of
older people. Certainly, among the older members of our
community the interplay of mind and body and spirit
often determines the tone and quality of life in the declining years. Added to the normal demands of active
adults living in the community, there is the superimposed
demand among aging persons of conserving their remaining resources to meet the needs of a lengthened life.

Health and Aging

Aging must be viewed as an evolutionary process and not
as a disease. The need to play, to work within reasonable
limits, and to participate in group activities becomes more
urgent as family and business responsibilities lessen. The
ability to engage in these sustaining activities often has its
roots in the early adult years, when chronic disease can be
detected in time to allow the individual to learn to live
with it and to enjoy life in spite of it. Every physician has
case records of vigorous men and women in their prime,
stricken with a chronic illness, who rehabilitated themselves and enjoyed many years of useful and contented living. What happens when chronic disease is neglected is
vividly registered on the welfare rolls of every city and
county; chronic illness is a determining factor in a high
percentage of these cases.

The health needs of older people are exceedingly complex and show great variability. To meet these needs, com-
munity-wide planning is just as essential as broad-scale
planning for child health services. Convalescent facilities
and rehabilitation are special problems that require combined operations of health, welfare, and educational
groups in the community.

An important resource that is often overlooked is the

public attitude toward the health needs of our older citizens. We must acquaint our citizens with these special problems. With knowledge comes understanding and support. Health planning for the aged must go hand in hand with health planning for adults with chronic diseases. Maximum exploitation of the real and unexplored capacities of our older people will pay rich dividends in the total health of the community.

Inactivity and loneliness are associated hardships faced by our older citizens who are forced to retire because of age. Disease or disability may be present, and in multiple array, but as long as one is able to perform the normal functions of life, adaptation is remarkable. Besides, modern science has made possible the prevention or postponement of premature symptoms of old age in many cases.

We rarely can cure these diseases or disabilities, but we can halt their progression. The older person may be diseased but not sick. He still can perform some activity. Therefore, essential services for the older person include programs of prevention, diagnosis, treatment, and rehabilitation.

Major Chronic Diseases and Disabilities

As the number one killer in New York State and the cause of much disability among older persons, heart disease deserves much consideration.

The state's heart disease control program is comparatively well developed, and includes activities for (a) the early detection of heart disease, (b) improved medical care for cardiac patients, (c) rehabilitation of cardiac housewives, and (d) research studies designed to obtain basic information about heart disease and its prevention and early detection.

The magnitude of the problem dictates that these activities be further expanded and new activities considered. Possible fields for action include: (1) studies of the epidemiology of coronary artery disease, (2) state grants-in-aid for the support of local cardiac clinics, and (3) additional units for the early detection of incipient heart disease.

More than half the cases of cancer reported in New York State occur in persons past the age of sixty years. Hence, all parts of the cancer control program benefit elderly people.

At the Roswell Park Memorial Institute, a well-rounded program of research, patient care, and professional education is being conducted.

The rest of the cancer control program also is well rounded, and includes public education, professional education, detection centers, tumor clinics, and activities in cancer nursing.

Cerebral vascular accidents rank third in importance as a cause of death among persons past the age of forty years. Moreover, they result in one of the most common disabilities of older persons, namely hemiplegia.

The following public health activities should be undertaken in this area:

1. Studies of the factors that are responsible for cerebral vascular accidents, of the factors that influence the prognoses, and of the factors that determine the success or failure of rehabilitation activities.

2. Professional post-graduate educational activities for health workers (physicians, nurses, physiotherapists) concerned with the management of patients with hemiplegia.

3. Improved rehabilitation services that would handle patients with hemiplegia and its various complications. One field that deserves special consideration is the rehabilitation of persons with aphasia.

Despite the great prevalence of arthritis and rheumatism, these conditions have thus far been difficult to approach with public health techniques. There appears to be no state with a dynamic approach to the control of these diseases.

It is possible that the approach to arthritis and rheumatism control should be largely through an over-all effort in home care (nursing, physiotherapy). Much can be done, however, to prevent premature disability through professional education. Many hospitals and even some medical teaching centers in the state have either no facilities or entirely inadequate ones for physiotherapy. This is a possible field for action. One solution might be state grants-in-aid on a matching basis to develop facilities where they do not now exist.

Another possibility might be the development of a central reference center for complete evaluation and recommendations for the individual management of difficult cases of arthritis. Alternatively, this might be done regionally at the various medical centers.

Research activities should be a part of a comprehensive program.

Although the over-all incidence of tuberculosis has been decreasing, the average age of persons admitted to tuberculosis hospitals has been steadily increasing. Tuberculosis is becoming more and more a disease of older people, especially among males.

The entire tuberculosis control program, from case finding to rehabilitation, applies to all persons, including those advanced in years. Indeed, in 1953, approximately 31 per cent of all cases of tuberculosis were reported in people over the age of fifty-five years.

Nutritional deficiencies and inadequacies are more common among the aged than among any other group. Inactivity, diminished taste acuity, long-standing habits of poor food selection, and a growing tendency to take up food fads are all characteristic of the aging process, and frequently lead to malnutrition.

Accidents rank high among the major causes of death in New York State; they also exact a tremendous toll in permanent and temporary disability. In considering factors that affect the health of older persons, one cannot overlook the facts that almost one-third of all deaths from accidents occur among people over the age of sixty-five and that the accident rates for this group are the highest of all age groups. Older people are more susceptible to accidents than are younger persons.

Although diabetes may develop at any age, it is a disease that is more common among older persons. It is most frequent among the relatives of known diabetics, the obese, and those advancing in age. Of a group of 20,255 new cases of diabetes recently reported, 70 per cent were found in people over the age of forty years.

A comprehensive program for the control of diabetes should include the following components: (a) prevention, (b) early detection, (c) treatment, (d) follow-up, (e) professional education, (f) patient education, and (g) research.

Efforts should be made to delineate further the respective roles of local and state medical societies, local and state health departments, the Federal Public Health Service and the American Diabetes Association.

Osteoporosis probably occurs to some extent in all elderly people; it frequently produces disability, particularly in elderly women but also in men of markedly sedentary habits.

This is a condition that is frequently overlooked; that not infrequently is a cause of pain and disability among elderly persons; that can readily be detected by a simple screening procedure (X ray); that is amenable to improvement through the administration of available therapeutic procedures. Osteoporosis then lends itself to control through a public health approach.

There is general agreement among people in the dental public health field that the next major activity among dental programs should and will be concerned with periodontal disease. It is difficult to measure precisely the prevalence of the several disease processes which attack the periodontal tissues, including bone and surrounding soft tissues. It is well established, however, that these conditions account for more tooth loss among the aged than does dental decay. Those concerned with custodial care for the aged are well aware of the difficulty in maintaining the nutritional status of these people when they have lost many of their teeth.

Education for Optimum Health

To promote optimum health and prevent premature disablement among the older people, it is necessary to provide various medical services including screening, diagnosis, treatment, and rehabilitation. Rehabilitation would be functional, to enable an older person to make use of his existing capabilities. In addition to the medical services, there should be health education services to educate the aged in the care of their own health. The community also must be educated in a manner which would enable it to accommodate the older disabled person. Employers, in one case, might adjust their work patterns to accommodate older people who can work in a limited capacity. Families of older persons must learn how to care for these people and how to help them care for themselves.

Legislative bodies should be made aware that the older population is getting larger and should be cared for through special legislation and new facilities.

Community Programs

Professional groups must realize the needs of this older generation. The community must set up programs to provide not only work for older people but also means of recreation. Activities should include demonstrations of community programs and applied research in better use of personnel facilities. The West Haverstraw experiment, whereby we are making available one hundred beds for older people on welfare rolls, shows whether this group can be rehabilitated and given the opportunity to secure gainful employment. In addition to all this, there should be continued basic research in the cardiovascular heart diseases, arthritis, and other diseases which afflict the older person.

It is true that all of these programs continuously require money in large amounts. It is necessary, however, to extend these basic programs in health and welfare and to expand the diagnostic and research clinics. There also should be expansion in the chronic-disease hospitals, the rehabilitation centers, and nursing homes which care for the aged. We cannot expect state-wide programs to meet all the needs of the aged. Many problems should be solved on local levels. The biggest hurdle, at the moment, is that of getting government groups to shift from diagnosis and research to preventive services such as screening and health inventories, and to rehabilitation. It is true that these services require additional funds, but in the long run only they can relieve disability and disease in the older groups.

European Programs

These problems are being met in several countries in Europe. During the summer of 1954, it was my good fortune to visit Scandinavia to study this problem. In reviewing their methods I found that old age pensions, in principle, cover the whole population in all three countries, at age seventy in Norway, sixty-seven in Sweden, and sixty-five in Denmark. Sweden pays an old age pension to all persons, regardless of income, even to the King. Pensions are approximately $335 a year to a single person, and $530 to a married couple. Supplements for housing, clothing, and fuel are given to those with no other source of income. General taxation provides five-sixths of old age pension funds in Sweden and the entire amount in Denmark. Denmark's population in 1950 was slightly more than four million, of which 600,000 were sixty years of age or more. It is in this older group that most of the chronic diseases and disabilities occur.

Denmark gives single pensioners $320 a year in Copenhagen, $280 in provincial towns, and $240 in rural areas. For married couples these sums are increased by 50 per cent. The Danish old age pension, however, is reduced by 60 per cent of any private income exceeding one-half the old age pension. As a result, in Denmark less than three-fifths of all persons eligible receive it. Denmark supplements old age pensions for housing, clothing, and fuel. In addition, those who postpone the pension for two or more years receive a supplement. The total old age pension of a married couple with no private income equals about two-fifths of the earnings of an unskilled laborer, fully employed. Instead of taking a pension, the couple may elect care in special homes.

Old People's Homes

By 1953 there were more than 700 of these homes, appropriately called Old People's Homes, which were housing 16,000 of 255,000 old age pensioners in Denmark. The homes are erected by local authorities and although the largest of these serves 1,600 old age pensioners most of them are much smaller. Authorities consider that homes with seventy to one hundred beds are the most efficient type. In place of these homes the local authority may erect low-rent, old age pensioners' flats so that single or married people may live in their own communities and be near their friends and relatives. In visiting several of these flats, I found them to be modern in every respect. Denmark had, in 1952, more than 10,000 flats for old age pensioners with room for 12,500 persons. There is need, however, for a great many more since only about 5 per cent of old age pensioners are now in such flats. Copenhagen, for instance, has 5,000 flats to care for 6,110 old age pensioners. The rent is about $4.00 for a single person and $5.00 for a double per month.

Denmark's largest hospital and nursing home for old people, De Gamles By, is in Copenhagen and is under the direction of Dr. T. Geill, who has specialized in diseases and disabilities of old people. The hospital has a staff of seven full-time doctors, seven part-time doctors, one part-time specialist in physical medicine, one pathologist, and seven physiotherapists. Of the 1,600 beds in this home, 500 are hospital beds, 300 are nursing beds, and 800 are for old age pensioners whether well or sick. The per capita cost per day at this hospital is about $7.00 for acutely ill patients and $2.50 for other beds. Heart diseases seemed to be the main problem, according to Doctor Geill, who does about 500 post-mortems a year to study the termination of his cases thoroughly.

The newer section of De Gamles By contains all new flats where a single old age pensioner may live in one room and a married couple in two rooms. There are bathing facilities on each floor. Occupants can have meals in the room and visit guests in lounges on each floor. The pensioners may provide their own chairs, radios, and pictures but a good bed is furnished by the home. On the average, the age of the males in this hospital is seventy-six and for the women, seventy-eight. The pensioners may work in the garden and kitchen, if they wish, earning token payments for spending money. The home provides a large library, concert hall, and exercise yard. Pensioners may come and go as they wish and are permitted to visit relatives for one month. They are given an allowance of money for fourteen days each year to help pay their board when they are visiting.

Doctor Geill prefers units of eighty to one hundred beds for old age pensioners when it is possible to build new units. The flexibility of having hospital, infirmary, and flats available at one place is favored by Doctor Geill, who also would like to see flats spread throughout the city so that the old people can be near their families and friends. Such a unit is a thirty-bed apartment unit for old age pensioners in the suburb of Lillerad, where the community has tried to place people near their friends and relatives.

Sweden's first home for the aged, erected in 1752, is located at Sabbatsberg in the city of Stockholm, about fifteen minutes' drive from the center of the city. It is used today as part of the Public Assistance Authority program of care for aged persons with diseases or disabilities and includes also a nursing home for 370 geriatric patients.

The 300 or more patients admitted each year include some frail old people who cannot live alone because they need nursing care. These people, who need minor medical care, also require help in dressing, eating, and making beds. The Institution has a special seventy-four–bed unit for this group.

Physical therapy and occupational therapy are used extensively and are highly valued both by this hospital staff and patients. Participation in occupational therapy helps pass the time and makes the old people feel they are still able to do something with their hands. Most of these patients are pensioners who can pay fixed costs out of their allotments. Although those in the Hospital for the Aged give up their pensions, they do receive about twelve dollars a month for pocket money.

Dr. S. Erlandsson, the Chief Medical Officer at Sabbatsberg, has two full-time staff doctors, two physical therapists, and one occupational therapist with an assistant. There is one nurse for every forty beds in the hospital, one for sixty in the unit for frail people and one nurse for every 110 patients in the Home for the Aged. The staff attempts at the outset to get the old age patients out of bed. For this purpose, a special low bed is provided, the mattress of which comes up to the kneecap of the average older person, facilitating its use. Falls and fractures are uncommon with such beds. Most of the injuries and cerebral accidents occur in the bathroom, according to Dr. Erlandsson. The staff refrains from performing any unneeded tasks for old age patients. In this manner, the older people learn to help themselves.

Dr. Erlandsson is impressed again and again by the learning ability of many of these older people, who are often in their eighties. They learn a new language, how to use the left hand if the right becomes paralyzed and how to occupy themselves with weaving, knitting, and sewing. All these things help to keep up their spirits. If expert geriatric diagnosis is combined with therapy, one can often rehabilitate the aged even though they cannot be cured of their troubles. Where there is understanding, patience, and compassion and not just sympathy, pity, or tolerance, life can be made pleasant in the twilight years even for those who are ill as well as aged.

The county governments in Sweden have the responsibility for hospital care, including that for older people. The Royal Social Board has jurisdiction over the old people's homes and the Royal Medical Board over mental cases among the older people. The Royal Social Board has charge of medical care of older people, but has no physicians on its staff. The State Pension Board has a separate program for all ages but sends no patients to homes for the aged.

All Norwegians who reach seventy years of age are entitled to old age pensions, the expenses of which come from local authorities and a 1 per cent state tax on yearly income of all taxpayers. The Invalidity Fund takes care of the blind and the crippled.

In Oslo, the main hospital for care of older people with chronic diseases and disabilities is the Ulleval Hospital. It has 180 beds for chronic disease and disability, 110 for females, and 70 for males. Sixty per cent of admissions come from old age homes, and 40 per cent are transfers from general hospitals in the city. Some come from nursing homes and others from psychiatric units for the aged. The geriatrics department is directed by Dr. Victor Gaustad, a professor on the staff of the Medical School of the University of Oslo, who believes that 40 beds are optimum capacities for an old people's nursing home. Doctor Gaustad's main task is providing nursing care for the old people, and his principal medical work is examination and placement of patients, whose average stay is three months. He uses male nurses in addition to female nurses.

There also are a number of private nursing homes in Oslo subsidized by the state, which provide 1,700 beds; 291 of these are associated with old age homes. Some are privately run for profit and not all are up to high standards of care. During 1955 Oslo plans to add 450 beds for old people to existing hospitals by converting old epidemic hospitals, no longer needed for that purpose. The city has, also, 1,200 apartments for old people similar to those described for Sweden and Denmark and plans to provide 2,000 more in the near future.

Health and welfare centers for out-patient services for the elderly are being planned throughout Oslo, and it is hoped that in this way as many patients as possible will be kept out of hospitals and nursing homes. Ambulatory examinations and classification, and aftercare, will then be given by teams of doctors, physical and occupational therapists, and social workers. There are three such centers now in operation experimentally with the support of the National Association to Combat Tuberculosis. The director of this association, Dr. Tobias Gedde-Dahl said that the association will expand into this type of work as tuberculosis decreases in importance. He already has set up a Division of Gerontology to study and explore problems associated with the aging process. Individuals serving as "home helpers" are provided to avoid hospital care and nursing-home care. An old person who cannot prepare food at home can come to the center and get food three times a day or, in some cases, food may even be brought to the home. Volunteers assist in the whole project, which includes club and recreational activities. This policy to regionalize and decentralize all services for old people even within a large city has great possibilities both for effectiveness and satisfaction to all concerned.

Socialization of health, education, and welfare services in the Scandinavian countries has made possible some interesting patterns of rehabilitation and geriatric services. Although it would not be realistic at the present time to pattern chronic disease and disability services in the United States after those in Scandinavia because of different governmental structures and cultural backgrounds, there are many things we can adapt to our programs.

Pilot Study at New York State Rehabilitation Hospital

One step taken by New York State in this problem has been the establishment of a pilot study at the New York State Rehabilitation Hospital in West Haverstraw for the evaluation and rehabilitation of disabled persons receiving public welfare assistance.

The hospital has been used to rehabilitate disabled children, including those crippled by poliomyelitis. With the increase in the older population and the higher incidence of disability within this group coupled with the expected drop in paralytic polio cases in the future, one hundred beds were set aside at the hospital for this study.

The objectives of this pilot study are twofold: (1) to determine the extent to which application of modern rehabilitative techniques can restore self-sufficiency to disabled persons on public assistance; and (2) to develop more efficient techniques for rehabilitation of disabled adults and to obtain information on costs, personnel, and special hospital facilities required.

Sponsored by the Department of Health and the Department of Social Welfare, the program accepted its first patient in April. Those patients approved for admission to

the hospital by its staff will be admitted for evaluation for
a period of three weeks at no charge to the local department of public welfare. The elimination of charge during
the evaluation period is suggested as an encouragement
to local welfare commissioners to participate in the study.

During the evaluation a complete diagnostic work-up
will be performed, including evaluation of activities of
daily living; and following this, the rehabilitation team
decides the patient's rehabilitation potential. Records are
kept in such a form as to permit analysis on a predetermined basis and objective comparison with the patient's
status after the patient had undergone rehabilitation at
this or another hospital, and at intervals subsequent to
discharge.

Only ten patients are being evaluated at any one time
but the case load will be increased gradually as the hospital staff gains experience and as standard procedures
are developed. For those patients who will actually
undergo treatment and rehabilitation, a charge of five
dollars a day will be made on the local welfare department
referring the patient. This should not hinder the program
since local welfare departments have to pay an average of
five dollars a day for the care of patients in nursing and
convalescent homes.

Each patient will be given the full range of treatment
in accordance with the rehabilitation plan worked out during the evaluation period. All types of therapy available
at the hospital will be used in accordance with the patient's needs. The hospital services will carry out prevoca-
tional testing, training, and guidance for those patients
having a potential for full-time or part-time employment.

A regular follow-up program will be established with
the local welfare department which referred the patient.

In this manner the benefits of the techniques can be studied and evaluated over a considerable period of time.

Techniques of Prevention and Care by Public and Private Physicians

In reviewing this and other programs for our country, it is necessary that, to insure health and peace of mind to our old persons, the private and public health physicians contribute techniques of prevention and care. These should properly include the early discovery of disease processes through periodic examinations that start in middle life and continue for one's remaining years. By such means many cases of chronic disease, with all their agony and sure fatality, might either be prevented or, through the substitution of different living methods, be rendered tolerable.

Treatment, promptly and adequately provided, should be made available the moment disablement of any character is detected. Geriatric services for both diagnosis and treatment need expansion. Re-ablement services that teach the sick to live within the limits of their physical and mental liabilities should be universally undertaken for the old as well as for the stricken young. Rehabilitation helps to prevent many aged people from becoming helpless and bedridden.

There are several check-points which can be established. The West Haverstraw program could be expanded so that all old people on public assistance could be evaluated for disablement and possible rehabilitation. The program could be co-ordinated with state rehabilitation hospitals and crippled children's hospitals. The many tuberculosis sanitoria which will no longer be needed could be established as rehabilitation centers.

Older patients admitted to general hospitals could be evaluated for disability and possible rehabilitation. This would serve as a check-point for those who are not on public assistance but are disabled. The precedent for such a program has been established in New York State where general hospitals, in co-operation with the State Health Department, make chest X rays of all patients admitted, for the purpose of screening out tuberculosis. All that is needed is simply a variation and extension of this established and well-accepted procedure.

Economic cares and fears that blight the mental and spiritual lives of so many of our older men and women are related problems for which the public is responsible. Without freedom from worry, the comfort and calm which should be the heritage of the aged are rarely achieved. Geriatrics and gerontology are fields which particularly invite the co-operation of private and public-health physicians. An increasingly large segment of our aging population needs our help. In giving it, we can do much to alleviate the rigors and unnecessary suffering of old age. Granting the aged their health rights offers the hope of greater happiness, serenity, and dignity to their lives.

Emerging Concepts

Part II

FUTURE TRENDS
IN OUR OLDER
POPULATION *Chapter IV*

HENRY D. SHELDON

Henry D. Sheldon, Ph.D., Washington, D.C., is chief of the Demographic Statistics Branch of the Population and Housing Division, Bureau of the Census, U.S. Department of Commerce. He has served as statistician with primary responsibilities for data on age, sex, race, nativity, and migration in the 1950 Census of Population and Housing and in the Current Population Survey.

THE POPULATION sixty-five years old and over in 1950—about twelve million—was roughly four times as large as the corresponding population in 1900. By the year 2000, a population of twenty-seven million in this age group, twice as large as that of 1950, is implied by the assumptions underlying the most recent projection issued by the Bureau of the Census. This figure suggests that the rate of growth in the older population will be somewhat less in the last half than in the first half of this century.

The Role of Births

Fundamentally the general dimensions of the population sixty-five years old and over, or for that matter the population of any given age group, are set by the number of births in an appropriate earlier period. Thus, the population sixty-five years old and over in 1950 represents the survivors of births in the period 1860 to 1885, and the older population in 2000, births in the period 1910 to 1935. This general relationship is indicated by the ratios of increase for both births and the population sixty-five and over presented in Table I. Here changes in the magnitude of the number of births, period by period, are roughly paralleled by changes in the size of the older population at appropriate later dates.

Births, Deaths, and Immigration

Some general notion of the contribution of the several factors accounting for the increase in our older population can be obtained by the use of crude census survival rates relating the estimated number of births to the native population sixty-five to eighty-nine years old. On this basis about 15 per cent of the births between 1810 and 1835 survived to be sixty-five to eighty-nine years old in 1900. The corresponding figure for the 1950 population sixty-five to eighty-nine years old was 21 per cent. If the survival rate for 1900 (15 per cent) is applied to the births contributing to 1950 native population sixty-five to eighty-nine a rough estimate of what the size of that population would have been had there been no decline in mortality is possible. A comparison of this figure (6.5 million) with the observed figure for 1900 (2.1 million) gives some indication of the increase attributable to the greater number of births (4.4 million).

Conversely, an application of the survival rate for 1950 (21 per cent) to the births contributing to the 1900 native population sixty-five to eighty-nine gives an estimate of what the size of the 1950 population would have been had there been no increase in the number of births but the observed improvement in mortality had occurred. A comparison of this figure (about 3.1 million) with that ob-

Table I

POPULATION 65 YEARS OLD AND OVER AND ESTIMATED NUMBER OF BIRTHS CONTRIBUTING TO THIS POPULATION FOR THE UNITED STATES: 1900 TO 2000

(Population data for 1900 adjusted for unknown age)

| Year | Population | | | | Estimated number of births contributing to population of specified dates [1] | | | | | Period of birth | |
| | All ages (thousands) | 65 years old and over | | | All ages (thousands) | 65 years old and over | | | All ages | 65 years and over |
		Number (thousands)	Per cent of all ages	Ratio of number to that of previous date		Number (thousands)	Per cent of all ages	Ratio to previous date		
1900........	75,995	3,088	4.1	—	120,200	14,300	11.9	—	1810–1900	1810–1835
1950........	150,697	12,270	8.1	4.0	218,400	44,200	20.2	3.1	1860–1950	1860–1885
Projections:										
1975 A [2]......	220,982	20,689	9.4	1.7	281,400	60,700	21.6	1.4	1885–1975	1885–1910
B [3]......	213,568	20,689	9.7	—	273,800	60,700	22.2	—	—	—
C [4]......	206,615	20,689	10.0	—	266,700	60,700	22.8	—	—	—
D [5]......	198,632	20,689	10.4	—	258,600	60,700	23.5	—	—	—
2000 [6]........		26,500	—	1.3	—	69,500	—	1.1	1910–2000	1910–1935

1 Estimated. Strictly speaking the number of births are those which contribute to the population under 90 years old and the population 65 to 89 years old on the specified dates. Since in 1950 persons 90 years old and over constituted about 0.1 per cent of the total population and about 1 per cent of the population 65 years old and over, and since the estimates of births are subject to an appreciable margin of error, the lack of exact correspondence between age and period of birth is inconsequential.

2 Assumes 1950–53 fertility level continues to 1975.

3 Assumes 1950–53 fertility level continues to 1965 and then declines to about the 1940 level by 1975.

4 Assumes 1950–53 fertility level declines from 1953 to about the 1940 level by 1975.

5 Assumes 1950–53 fertility level declines from 1953 to about the 1940 level by 1960 and continues at that level to 1975.

6 Estimated number of persons 65 years old and over would constitute about 10 per cent of a total population of 275 million.

SOURCE: 1950 Population Census, Vol. II *Characteristics of the Population; Current Population Reports,* Series P-25, No. 78; and unpublished estimates.

served for 1900 (about 2.1 million) suggests the probable gain from declining mortality (about 1.0 million).

If from the total increase in the native population sixty-five to eighty-nine between 1900 and 1950 (7.3 million) we take the gain attributable solely to the greater number of births (4.4 million) and that attributable solely to the decline in mortality (about 1.0 million), the residual (about 2.0 million) represents the gain arising jointly from declining mortality and increasing births; that is, the decline in mortality among the 30 million births by which births between 1860 and 1885 exceeded those occurring between 1810 and 1835.

The results of these calculations presented in Table I-A indicate that about 48 per cent of the increases is attributable to the greater number of births, about 10 per cent to declining mortality, 22 per cent to the greater number of births and declining mortality, and 19 per cent to immigration. The amount attributed to immigration is simply the increase in the foreign-born population sixty-five to eighty-nine years old and thus includes whatever increase which might be attributed to improved mortality in this segment of the population.

Table I-A

COMPONENT OF INCREASE IN THE POPULATION
65 TO 89 YEARS OLD: 1900 TO 1950

Components	Number (thousands)	Per cent
Total	9,067	100
Native	7,317	81
Increase in number of births	4,389	48
Decline in mortality	949	10
Decline in mortality among excess births	1,979	12
Foreign-born (immigration)	1,750	19

If the assumptions under which the figure for the year 2000 was derived are correct, then the rate of immigration and declining mortality may be somewhat less important in the next 50 years. The assumptions imply an annual complement of net immigration of 200,000 to 250,000, a figure which is relatively low in comparison to early decades of this century. At the present writing there seems to be little reason to question this assumption.

On the other hand the projections assume no improvement in mortality after the period 1955 to 1960. This assumption would seem to imply that most of the possible reductions in mortality have been made. At the other extreme we have optimistic predictions, extrapolating the results of current medical research, of life expectations running well above 100 years. To the best of my knowledge these predictions are impressionistic, and are not based on life tables constructed from projected mortality rates nor do they specify the date at which the predicted expectation will be achieved. On balance, it would appear that the role of declining mortality is somewhat understated, and thus the size of the older population—to what extent, however, remains an open question. Various projections of life expectation appear in Table II.

Relative Position of the Aged

For many purposes figures on the total population sixty-five and over are adequate, but if we are viewing with alarm the shift toward the upper age levels, then it is necessary to consider the older population as a proportion of the population of all ages. Here again the fundamental dimensions are set by the temporal pattern in the number of births prior to the date under consideration. In Table I, the number of births which accounts for the older population is expressed as a percentage of the number of births

Table II

EXPECTATION OF LIFE FOR WHITE MALES AND
FEMALES, FOR THE UNITED STATES:
1900, 1950, AND 1955 TO 1960

Year	At birth			At age 65		
	Male	Female	Differ- ence	Male	Female	Differ- ence
1900 to 1902.........	48.2	51.1	2.9	11.5	12.2	0.7
1949 to 1951.........	66.3	72.0	5.7	12.8	15.0	2.2
1955 to 1960:						
"High" mortality....	66.6	72.6	6.0	12.6	14.8	2.2
"Medium" mortality.	67.7	74.2	6.5	12.7	15.3	2.6
"Low" mortality....	69.6	77.0	7.4	13.1	16.3	3.2
1970...............	69.8	76.4	6.6	—	—	—

SOURCE: Bureau of Census: *United States Life Tables and Actuarial Tables, 1939 to 1941, Current Population Reports,* Series P-25, No. 43.
National Office of Vital Statistics, *United States Life Tables, 1949 to 1951.*
Harold F. Dorn: "Prospects of Further Decline in Mortality Rates," *Human Biology,* December, 1952, Vol. 24, No. 4.

which accounts for the total population at the specified dates, and, here again, the changes in these percentages parallel the corresponding changes in the per cent sixty-five and over. In general the increase in these percentages reflects the declining birth rate in the period 1810 to 1940.

In the case of the proportion of older persons the effects of improved mortality and of migration are by no means so clear. To be sure, both these factors increased the size of the population sixty-five and over in 1950 over what might have been expected if the conditions prior to 1900 had prevailed. They also contributed, however, to the population under sixty-five both directly and indirectly in terms of natural increase. Thus it is by no means clear that either declining mortality or immigration actually increased the proportion of older persons between 1900 and 1950.

In hazarding a guess as to the proportion of the population sixty-five and over in the year 2000, the primary concern is with the size of the population under sixty-five as of that date. Kingsley Davis, in a recent article, has committed himself to a total figure of 275 million although he concedes 300 million might be possible.[1] The percentage sixty-five and over with these totals would be 9.6 and 8.8 respectively, figures not appreciably different from the Series A figure for 1975. Assumption of declining fertility, of course, would lead to higher percentages. Currently there is no evidence of a drop in the fertility level below that of the 1950 to 1953 period; in fact, estimates of the actual population are running ahead of the projections. If this situation were to continue to the end of the century it is conceivable that the proportion of population sixty-five and over might well be below that of 1950. In any event it seems improbable that there will be an increase in this proportion anywhere near the size of that observed between 1900 and 1950.

Predominance of Women

The increase in the number and proportion of older persons between 1900 and 1950 has been accompanied by an increase in the proportion of women in this population. In 1900 there were actually more men than women sixty-five and over; in 1950 there were nine men for every ten women; and by 1975, projections indicate roughly seven men for every ten women. On this basis, there would be some 3 million more women than men (Table III).

[1] Kingsley Davis, " 'Ideal Size' for Our Population," *The New York Times Magazine*, May 1, 1955, p. 12.

Table III

POPULATION 65 YEARS OLD AND OVER, BY SEX, FOR THE
UNITED STATES: 1900, 1950, 1960, and 1975

Year	Total	Male	Female	Males per 100 females
TOTAL POPULATION				
1900[1]........	3,088,368	1,560,382	1,527,986	102.1
1950.........	12,269,537	5,796,974	6,472,563	89.6
Projections:				
1960A[2]......	15,701,000	7,079,000	8,622,000	82.1
1975A[2]......	20,689,000	8,701,000	11,988,000	72.6
NATIVE POPULATION				
1900[1]........	2,133,043	1,063,018	1,070,025	99.3
1950[3]........	9,538,231	4,403,080	5,135,151	85.7

[1] Adjusted for unknown age.
[2] Including armed forces overseas.
[3] Ratio estimate based on 20 per cent sample.
    SOURCE: 1950 Population Census: Vol. II, *Characteristics of the Popu-lation.* Bureau of the Census, *Current Population Reports,* Series P-25, No. 78.

Although some part of this change is attributable to the decline in the volume of immigration, in which, historically, men have predominated, it is largely a matter of the lower mortality rates among women. This difference, which existed at the beginning of this century, has increased progressively since that time. In 1900, for example, the expectation of life for white females exceeded that for white males by 2.9 years. By 1950 this difference had increased to 5.7 years, and assuming a continuation of past trends it will increase to 6.5 years in the period 1955 to 1960. Although it is possible that this trend may be reversed and the gap between male and female mortality narrowed, there is no evidence of such a development at the present writing.

When to this increasing excess of women at the older ages, which arises from differential mortality, we add the fact that wives on the average are younger than their husbands, and the fact that widowers tend to remarry more frequently than widows, it appears that widowhood may well be one of the major problems in the field of aging.

Shift in the Dependency Ratio

The ratio of persons in the dependent ages,—that is, the very young and the very old,—to the population of working age has frequently been taken as indicative of the extent to which the age structure favors an excess of production over consumption. The working population has sometimes been defined as that aged 20 to 64 years, and the remaining extremes as the dependent population. Data on the trend in these ratios are presented in Table IV. It is clear that the trend in the total ratio is in large part a function of the trend in the ratio of children to persons of working age. There was a steady decline in the total from 1,113 per thousand in 1870 to 702 per thousand in 1940, which generally paralleled the ratio for children. In the decade 1940 to 1950, the rise in the ratio for older persons brought the total ratio up slightly; but thereafter the sharp rise in the total ratio is in large part a result of the high level of fertility assumed in the A series. It is noteworthy that if the D series is used (that is, the assumption that fertility will revert to roughly the 1940 level by 1960 and continue at that level thereafter) the total ratio for 1975 is not materially higher than that for 1950. In short, although the ratio of older persons to working population has increased steadily throughout the period under consideration, it still constitutes the minor part of the total ratio. It would be the determining element in the total ratio only in the case of a population which was not replacing itself or conceivably a population for which the main source of increase was the in-migration of adults.

Table IV

DEPENDENCY RATIOS, FOR THE UNITED STATES: 1870 TO 1975

Year	Population 20 to 64 years old	Dependent population			Ratio: number per 1,000 20 to 64 years		
		Total	65 years and over	Under 20 years	Total	65 years and over	Under 20 years
1870[1]........	18,243,358	20,309,852	1,153,649	19,156,203	1113	63	1050
1900[1]........	39,032,419	36,761,572	3,080,498	33,681,074	942	79	863
1940..........	77,344,357	54,324,918	9,019,314	45,305,604	702	117	586
1950[2]........	87,680,000	63,452,000	12,269,000	51,183,000	724	140	584
Projections:							
1960 A[2].....	94,469,000	82,957,000	15,701,000	67,256,000	878	166	712
1975 A[2].....	115,251,000	105,731,000	20,689,000	85,042,000	917	180	738
D[2]......	114,868,000	83,764,000	20,689,000	63,075,000	729	180	549

[1] Excluding persons of unknown age.
[2] Including armed forces overseas.

SOURCE: Hearings before a subcommittee of the Committee on Ways and Means, House of Representatives, 83rd Congress, First Session on United States Population Trends and Tax Treatment of Individuals under Private Pension Plans, Part 2, Table II.

Summary

In summary then, we have examined the implications of current demographic trends as they relate to the growth and characteristics of the older population in the latter half of the twentieth century. This consideration has led to the conclusion that by the end of the century a population sixty-five and over of 25 to 30 million may be expected,—about twice the size of the current population of this age. The proportion of the population sixty-five and over in 2000 will depend on fertility trends in the next forty-five years, but may reasonably be expected not to vary by more than a few percentage points from that observed in 1950. The decline in the sex ratio at the upper ages may be expected to continue so that by 1975 women sixty-five and over may outnumber men of the same age by 3 million. The dependency ratio may be expected to rise particularly if high fertility levels are assumed. In fact the trends in the total ratio would appear to depend more on changes in fertility than on changes in the size of the older population.

THE COMING
ECONOMIC CHALLENGE
OF LONGEVITY *Chapter V*

ALLEN W. RUCKER

> *Allen W. Rucker is president of the Eddy-Rucker-Nickels Company, Management Consultants, in Cambridge, Massachusetts. His firm serves industries in the United States, Canada, and Europe. His publications include* Share of Production Wage Plan, Labor's Road to Plenty, Scientific Price Management, *and various articles.*

PROBABLY your first introduction to economics, as was mine, came through this little rhyme used by our mothers and fathers:

> Eat it up, wear it out;
> Make it do or do without.

Condensed into these twelve words is the essence of dealing with scarcities by economizing. Economizing is not necessary unless there are scarcities, and of course there are no "economics" concerned when we breathe air or look at the morning sun. When we come to food, clothing, housing, and the amenities of life, however, we come to scarcities, to economizing, and to the economic facts of life. These are formidable enough during the working years of most of us; when we retire they tend to become far more so. When millions of individuals, men and women alike, face this same problem we have an economic chal-

lenge that cannot be ignored. Let me first sketch briefly
the outlines of this challenge.

Just now our senior citizens number more than 12.5
million, a number greater than the population of metropolitan New York City. By 1960 our seniors will number
more than 15 million; by 1975, our number will be 21
million.[1]

The Rising Costs of Dependency

What does this mean in economic terms? Perhaps the easi-
est answer is to assume that our senior citizens will want
an average yearly income equal to the present per capita
average income of all Americans, about $2,200 in 1954
dollars. On that basis, assuming no further inflation of the
cost of living, the economic sustenance of our senior citizens currently comes to about 27.5 billion dollars; in 1960
it will be approximately 33 billion dollars; and in 1975
approximately 50 billion dollars. As the years pass, these
sums rise to and then exceed the present cost of national
defense.

If none of our senior citizens was self-supporting, $50
billion would be the estimated economic burden on our
working population in 1975. This $50 billion means the
total cost in 1954 prices. As I shall show later, we can expect that sum to rise to $82 billion or more because of
continuous price inflation. A little later on, I shall come
back to this vital factor. First, however, let us note the
following points. To the extent that individuals over sixty-
five years are self-supporting, the approximate cost of
longevity will be self-financing. As nearly as I can determine, about one-fourth and just possibly as many as
one-third may be wholly self-sustaining. This means that
three-fourths or maybe two-thirds are forced to depend

[1] See Chapter IV for more detailed population projections.

in whole or part upon their families or upon the public for the means of existence. The majority of these will be women, for the ladies have proved themselves to be far and away the "better halves" in the matter of living and longevity.

Here, then, is the economic problem and the economic challenge of longevity; but there is another side to it which we cannot ignore. We must go behind the dollar sign to the food, the clothing, the housing, and the good things of life—to the quantities of these things which must be produced and made available to our senior citizens, regardless of the amount of money involved.

Our senior citizens are not, however, and will never be the sole claimants to the production of the United States. Currently, we have about 44 million children under fifteen years of age who are nonself-supporting. Due to the acceleration in recent years of the birth rate, our under-working-age population is growing much faster than for some decades heretofore. With the present birth rate continued to 1975, we shall then have approximately 75 million youngsters under fifteen years of age.[2] When we add the number of our senior citizens who ought not to have to work to the number of our junior citizens, we have the total of those to be supported by our working population and our tools of production. Let us take a quick look at these totals:

Currently, our seniors are 12.5 million and our juniors 44 million, or a total of 56.5 million; 35 per cent of our entire population.

By 1975, our seniors will be 21 million and our juniors 75 million, or a total of 96 million; 45 per cent of our estimated population twenty years hence.

This enormous coming increase in the nonself-supporting population, an increase of 40 million seniors and juniors within twenty years, will be a unique and unprece-

[2] See Chapter IV for additional figures on the dependency ratio.

dented development in our national history. That number represents more people than we had in all age groups at the time General Grant was President. It is equal to the present population of all six New England States, plus Ohio, Indiana, Illinois, Michigan, and Wisconsin.

Can We Produce Enough?

Can we produce enough food, clothing and other good things to maintain and to increase the scale of living of all of these people?

Can we manage to distribute equitably what we produce, so that our senior citizens, as well as the youngsters, can look forward to the future with hope and contentment?

Let us consider briefly some of the factors that bear on these two questions.

What about production? Everything that people expect to live on and to enjoy during their declining years must be produced by their tools and the working population. They also must produce adequately for the rapidly expanding number of their juniors as well as for themselves. What is the outlook?

For the past forty years manufacturing output has been expanding at an average rate of 4.1 per cent yearly, compounded. That increase was shared by an average population growth of 1.1 per cent, so that the per capita gain in the scale of living amounted to an average of about 3.0 per cent yearly, also compounded. In other words, Americans have become accustomed not only to a high scale of living but also to a steady improvement year after year. This latter fact largely accounts for our relative political stability and comparative freedom from "isms" which infect almost every other nation on the globe. It is not so much the level of our living but the vital fact that the level is steadily rising which is vital to our future.

But will a production increase of 4.1 per cent yearly be

enough to maintain this rate of improvement in the future? Probably not. The reasons briefly are these: first, our total population is growing faster by two-fifths than before; second, the number of our senior citizens is increasing much faster than heretofore. In addition, our working population, especially those between the most productive ages of twenty and fifty, will not begin to grow in proportion to the population for more than a decade to come, if by then. In other words, we face one and perhaps two decades in which the number of man-hours of labor available relative to population will be definitely below past experience.

Nor is this all. Our total manufacturing product, according to my studies, increases in direct proportion to two factors, (a) the tools of production and (b) the total man-hours of labor used. Over the past forty years, we have increased our investment in tools about 3 per cent yearly, compounded, and our total man-hours of work in industry about 1.1 per cent yearly, causing a total of 4.6 per cent annual increase in output.

There is little likelihood that we can accelerate the increase in the man-hours of work applied during the next decade or two. We must remember, as Peter Drucker points out, that all the people who will go to work in the next twenty years have already been born. We must also remember that there is a constant pressure to reduce the number of working hours per person at work. We probably cannot count upon stepping up the annual increase in man-hours of work for ten to twenty years to come.

That forces our attention upon increasing the quality and quantity of tools of production at a faster rate than the past forty-year average of 3.0 per cent yearly. The more far-sighted of our industrial leaders see this; note, as one example, the recent step-up to 2 billion dollars in the expansion program of General Motors. Far too few industrialists and far too few of our citizens have yet grasped the fact that we shall need, year after year, a total added investment in manufacturing alone almost a third greater than our past average, if we are to meet the economic challenge of longevity.

Our future rate of capital growth should be more than 3.0 per cent yearly and probably 3.5 per cent to 4.0 per cent for the indefinite future.

Here is a field of interest and personal endeavor in which our citizens, especially our senior citizens, may well enter—even if only to show, demonstrate, and educate young and old alike to the imperative need for ever-greater capital accumulation in industry. The amount of and the ease with which we can obtain the food, the housing, the clothing, and the amenities of life for our later years will depend upon a sharp acceleration of the growth of tools of production. I have high confidence that we shall attain the production increases needed, especially if we seniors will use some of our time in cultivating a local and national political climate that will encourage individual saving and stimulate new investment and risk-taking.

The Question of Distribution

Granting that we can accelerate the increase in annual output, how shall it be distributed among our senior citizens? In an economy in which the necessities of living come to us in exchange for money, how can we assure adequate incomes to all senior citizens?

This is a problem which historically most of us have tackled individually. During our working years we are accustomed to earning income from personal effort, thus assuring ourselves of a continuing supply of goods and services that make up our scale of living. Many of us, if not most, have also foreseen the day when our personal earnings would diminish; we have therefore set aside or saved for our retirement. Our savings consist of life insurance, stocks and bonds, income-producing real estate, contributions to pension funds, and so on. Those voluntary accumulations of individual savings have largely found their way into capital for productive tools and facilities. In brief, the thrifty people of our nation have voluntarily provided the means of steadily expanding our national output and thereby provided for themselves an income for their own old age.[3]

The problem of distributing tomorrow's production equitably so as to provide adequately for our senior citizens is chiefly a problem of how much how many of us save today. We need vastly to enlarge the number of voluntary savers among those who are working now, and thereby enlarge tomorrow the number who are wholly or partly self-supporting from today's savings. By so doing, we tend to assure the capital growth that will provide the new and better tools of production we need tomorrow, and also to assure a widely diffused flow of income to those who will retire and semi-retire in the coming years. This is the time-honored voluntary system of the American republic.

I do not think that it can be replaced by a compulsory distribution of income without loss of individual dignity and independence, and perhaps the ultimate destruction of personal liberty. Whatever the merits of the Federal Old Age Benefit system, its basic moral defect is that it is compulsory and not voluntary. Its basic economic defect is that the payroll tax which finances it in part does not

[3] See Chapter VI for material on the assets of today's older population.

represent savings and capital accumulation. It contributes nothing to expanding the tools and equipment of industry and agriculture so imperatively needed to expand output for the future. Its basic political defect is yet to be exposed; it consists in taxing the working population to support those who no longer can work—and when that burden reaches the 50 to 80 billion dollars a year total, we shall see a tragic political cleavage: youth arrayed against age, son against father, and daughter against mother. Those three defects, moral, economic, and political, may well undermine this republic which we here now think we have bequeathed to our children and our grandchildren.

If we are to pass on to our descendants that heritage which we received from our forefathers, we senior citizens still have constructive patriotic work to do in the great field of promoting truly liberal ideas. These ideas of saving and thrift, independence and personal dignity in liberty are not exactly new, but they are nonetheless still genuinely liberal. Their antithesis, the concept of state compulsion, has neither the merit of being new nor the merit of being liberal. Liberality does not consist of making free with other people's money and freedom. Our senior citizens, and those of us who soon will be numbered among them, have still much to do in preserving the American heritage.

The Threat of Easy Money

I want to pin-point this opportunity and challenge in one highly specific way. Nearly every one of us knows, or soon will know, at first-hand what it means to live on a "fixed income." It means that so long as the inflationary expansion of our currency continues to force up the price level and the cost of living, those living on fixed incomes are inevitably condemned to a steadily declining scale of living. We are condemned to live on less and less each succeeding year.

Since this nation abandoned the dollar convertible into gold upon the demand of any citizen, the last practical restraint upon the unlimited issuance of paper money disappeared. Today, both major political parties are openly committed to the theory of a "steadily expanding money supply." Both parties have actually been following a policy of inflation since 1914.

That monetary policy finances federal deficits. Those deficits have the effect of pumping money into the economic system faster than we can increase the output of goods. Our manufacturing output increases at the average rate of 4.1 per cent yearly, whereas our money supply has an average rate of increase of 6.5 per cent yearly, compounded. This excess over output raises prices an average of 2.5 per cent yearly, compounded.

Seasoned businessmen and women will realize at once what this means. It means that the increasing productivity of the American system is not for those on fixed incomes, not for the elderly who earn little or no income from wages and salaries. It means an end to the natural tendency of higher productivity to lower costs and prices relative to incomes, thereby increasing the purchasing power of money. In this way, and only in this way can people on fixed incomes buy more each year; only in this way can our huge market among the senior citizens become an expanding market for industrial output. Only in this way could our senior citizens enjoy, along with other Americans, a rising scale of living. The monetary policy of the federal government, of both major political parties, denies them that opportunity. The aged and the elderly are not only denied an opportunity open to Americans of working age;

they are condemned by this "free-wheeling" monetary policy to suffer a continuous reduction in the purchasing power of their dollars.

To any thoughtful student of monetary history, ancient and modern alike, the deadliest enemy of the man and woman over sixty-five years old, is paper money that cannot be redeemed in gold on demand. Currently, over 12 million of our citizens are over sixty-five; by 1975, some 21 million will be in that age group. Most of today's senior citizens and those of tomorrow must live off a fixed income. The irredeemable dollar condemns them to accept a scale of living that will shrink about 2½ per cent yearly, compounded, as long as they live. This is the average annual rate at which paper money is forcing up the cost of living in this country.

To draw from personal experience, my father, on retirement in 1933, had lifetime savings which he thought ample for a comfortable living throughout his remaining life; but he was wrong. In that year, our government abandoned the gold standard and outlawed private possession of monetary gold. In ten years, each $1000 of my father's retirement income had shrunk to a purchasing power of $747. When he died in 1951, each $1000 of his fixed income was actually worth only $475 in terms of living costs. This was his reward for a lifetime of hard work, thrift, and prudence. Today, over 12 million others like him are receiving the same sort of reward.

Today's 12 million senior citizens will number 21 million in 1975. Some time between now and then, our senior citizens will represent the largest block of votes in the nation which can be mustered behind a single, crucial issue of how to avoid, or to halt their pauperization brought on by a flood of irredeemable paper money.

In the attempt to avoid, or to halt that process, the votes

of this politically superpowerful group of elderly citizens will be mustered by some future leader. They will force either a return to a dollar redeemable in gold, or, alternatively, they will force such an outpouring of more fiat money as a means of raising old age benefits, that well may topple the fiscal pillars of this republic. I do not pretend to know which way we shall vote; I do know that we 21 million will not submit in perpetuity to a sentence of pauperization from the depreciation in the purchasing power of our fixed incomes. Either we shall have to stop

Table I

SHRINKAGE IN PURCHASING POWER OF $1000 OF FIXED
INCOME AT RETIREMENT IN 1933

Year	Consumers' Price Index [1] (1947–49 = 100)	Index of Purchasing Power (1933 = 100) [2]	Purchasing Power of $1000
1933	55.3	100.0	$1000
1934	57.2	96.7	967
1935	58.7	94.2	942
1936	59.3	93.3	933
1937	61.4	90.1	901
1938	60.3	91.7	917
1939	59.4	93.1	931
1940	59.9	92.3	923
1941	62.9	87.9	879
1942	69.7	79.3	793
1943	74.0	74.7	747
1944	75.2	73.5	735
1945	76.9	71.9	719
1946	83.4	66.3	663
1947	95.5	57.9	579

[1] Index of the Bureau of Labor Statistics, U. S. Dept. of Labor.

[2] This Index adjusts the B.L.S. Index so that the year of retirement is taken as the base, or 100.0, in order to show the shrinkage in purchasing power of $1.00 of income. The conversion is made simply by dividing the B.L.S. Index for the starting year, 1933, by the Index of each subsequent year.

further inflation of the price level, or we shall have to force an inflation in our fixed incomes, equal to price inflation. It will be one or the other, and do not let any rationalization make you think otherwise. If you are now forty-five or fifty years old, you yourself will be among the 21 million of us voting to make one of these two forecasts come true.

Tables I and II show the depreciation in purchasing power of the dollar of fixed income. One shows what happened to a man who retired in 1933; the other shows what

Table II

SHRINKAGE IN PURCHASING POWER OF $1000 OF FIXED
INCOME AT RETIREMENT IN 1940

Year	Consumers' Price Index [1] (1947–49 = 100)	Index of Purchasing Power (1933 = 100) [2]	Purchasing Power of $1000
1940	59.9	100.0	$1000
1941	62.9	95.2	952
1942	69.7	85.9	859
1943	74.0	80.9	809
1944	75.2	79.7	797
1945	76.9	77.9	779
1946	83.4	71.8	718
1947	95.5	62.7	627
1948	102.8	58.3	583
1949	101.8	58.8	588
1950	102.8	58.3	583
1951	111.0	54.0	540
1952	113.5	52.8	528
1953	114.4	52.4	524
1954	114.8	52.2	522

[1] Index of the Bureau of Labor Statistics, U. S. Dept. of Labor.

[2] This Index adjusts the B.L.S. Index so that the year of retirement is taken as the base, or 100.0, in order to show the shrinkage in purchasing power of $1.00 of income. The conversion is made simply by dividing the B.L.S. Index for the starting year, 1940, by the Index of each subsequent year.

happened in fifteen years to the man who retired in 1940. This will demonstrate why 12 to 21 million senior Americans will one day politically combine to vote on this coming political issue—either to halt the decline in the purchasing power of their fixed incomes, or, to inflate their incomes in proportion to the inflation in the cost of living.

The Challenge

Here, I think, may be the greatest challenge to our senior citizens. The problem of expanding output to provide for a rising population of both youth and age is a great one; the problem of so encouraging saving as to diffuse income among the retired citizens of the future is an even greater one. The task of halting the inflation that well may beggar them in the last years of life is to me the greatest challenge of all.

This is the triple challenge now before us. Surely our mature judgment, our experience, and our courage offer the hope that we can meet it, that we can protect ourselves and build at the same time an impregnable foundation for the lives of those whom we proudly hail every day, our children and our grandchildren.

INCOME AND EMPLOYMENT:
BASIC FACTS *Chapter VI*

PETER O. STEINER

> *Peter O. Steiner, Ph.D., is assistant professor of economics, and research associate in the Institute of Industrial Relations at the University of California in Berkeley. Under a grant from the Rockefeller Foundation, he and his associates have made a study of the "Economic Implications of an Aging Population." His bibliography is extensive.*

THE FIVE-YEAR STUDY of the economic status of the aged undertaken at the Institute of Industrial Relations, University of California, under the financial sponsorship of the Rockefeller Foundation, demonstrates again the importance of research because the conclusions, as is often the case, differ from those anticipated upon the basis of initial preconceptions.

Much of the information upon which our study is based comes from a survey conducted for us in April, 1952 by the Bureau of the Census as a follow-up to the Current Population Survey of the same month. It was the first and, I believe, remains the only attempt to sample nationally the whole of the noninstitutional aged population. We believe our sample, containing about 3,600 aged individuals, to be representative of the population at that date. It is evident that important changes in the economic status of the aged have occurred since that date,[1] but I hope that

[1] See the article by Lenore Epstein, "Economic Resources of Persons Sixty-Five and Over," which appeared in the June, 1955, issue of the *Social Security Bull.*, for a discussion of those changes.

I have been at least qualitatively aware of them. Certain preliminary findings of the survey have been previously published.[2] A full report is near completion.

Survey Facts

The following appear to be among the demonstrated facts emerging from this survey that are relevant to the subsequent discussion:

1. Incomes of the aged are typically very low not only in absolute terms but relative to receipt requirements determined using developed budgets. A large group of the aged suffer from an acute receipt deficiency even when such factors as nonmonetary support and use of savings to meet living expenses are considered. This harsh conclusion is inescapable and is elsewhere documented.[3]

2. Differences among groups and among individuals with respect to incomes is very largely explained in terms of whether or not the individual (or couple) has earnings, and in terms of the size of those earnings. Certain summary comparisons are presented in Table I, but this conclusion rests as well upon a much more comprehensive analysis.

3. Differences in earnings, of course, reflect differences in the degree of labor force participation. Of the large group of the aged out of the labor force, however, only a small proportion can by the most earnest and enlightened efforts be brought back in. Put differently, the bulk of the nonemployed aged are not employable. This fact is so crucial, yet so little recognized, that I should like to quote briefly from the report of my colleague, Robert Dorfman:[4]

[2] *Amer. Economic Rev.*, May, 1954, pp. 634–70.
[3] Peter O. Steiner, "The Size, Nature, and Adequacy of the Resources of the Aged," *Amer. Economic Rev.*, May, 1954, pp. 645–55.
[4] Robert Dorfman, "The Labor Force Status of Persons Aged Sixty-Five and Over," *Amer. Economic Rev.*, May, 1954, pp. 635–36.

Table I

MEDIAN INCOME [1] OF AGED ECONOMIC UNITS
BY RECEIPT OF EARNINGS
1951

	Total	*Without Earnings*	*With Earnings*		
			Total	Earnings $1–499	Earnings $500 or More
Couples [2]					
1. Per cent of Couples...	100.0	43.3	56.7	12.5	44.2
2. Median Total Income..	$1387	$885	$2162	$580	$2695
Unrelated Males [3]					
1. Per cent of Unrelated Males	100.0	65.7	34.3	9.7	24.6
2. Median Total Income..	$ 662	$448	$1440	$431	$2029
Unrelated Females [3]					
1. Per cent of Unrelated Females	100.0	87.4	12.6	6.7	5.9
2. Median Total Income..	$ 273	$186	$ 738	$361	$1483

[1] Money income as defined by Bureau of the Census.

[2] A couple, the male member of which is 65 years or older. In 1952 there were approximately 3,800,000 aged couples.

[3] Aged individuals having no spouse, or with spouse absent. In 1952 there were approximately 1,800,000 unrelated males and 4,200,000 unrelated females 65 years or older.

SOURCE: *Follow-Up Survey,* April 1952.

. . . programs for reemploying older people, although they certainly may work constructively in many individual instances, cannot be expected to do much toward relieving the whole range of problems faced by the aged. Partly this is because 40 per cent of the men over sixty-four are already employed so that, insofar as employment is a cure for their problems, they are taken care of already. To a large extent this is because 77 per cent of the older men who are not in the labor force feel that they are not well enough to work. A re-employment program could hardly meet the needs of these men or their families. Finally, this is because the older members of the population have not only grown old; they have obsolesced. . . . The scope for programs of deferred retirement or for re-employment is appreciable. The survey revealed that

5 per cent of the men over sixty-five are not in the labor force but consider themselves well enough to work and would be interested in full- or part-time work. Five per cent of the 5.8 million men of sixty-five and over is not a contemptible number. Neither is it a solution to the complex of problems resulting from loss of employment status. . . .[5]

For women, employment prospects are even more remote. Sixty per cent of the women in our sample had not worked since they were fifty years old, i.e., since 1938 at the latest. Considering only the "unrelated females," about 10 per cent were in the labor force, 47 per cent lacked relevant work experience, 37 per cent were not well enough to work. Of the remaining 6 per cent many were not interested in working.

Some summary data are presented in Table II. Two final

Table II

SUMMARY ESTIMATES OF LABOR FORCE STATUS
APRIL 1952
(Thousands)

	Males	*Females*	*Total*
Persons 65 and over..............	5,760	6,520	12,280
In labor force...................	2,410	530	2,940
Not in labor force...............	3,350	5,990	9,340
Well enough to work.............	770		
Not well enough to work..........	2,580		
Well and interested in full- or part-time work	200	78	278

SOURCE: Population base from *Current Population Report,* page 20, No. 44. Percentage distributions from *Current Population Survey* for April 1952, and from follow-up survey.

comments on this point: first, it must be remembered that 1951 was characterized by a high level of employment and of cyclically ample job opportunities; the position of the

[5] See Chapter VII for further discussion of employment.

aged in the labor force will be appreciably *less* satisfactory in periods of even moderate unemployment. Second, the question may be asked about what "not well enough to work" means. About two-fifths of the group is composed of persons so obviously unable to work that Census enumerators are instructed to classify them as such without embarrassing them with questions, and three-fifths of persons who report themselves as too sick to do even occasional or part-time work. With respect to the latter, the Census experts report on the basis of detailed examination that such responses are overwhelmingly reliable indications of ill health.

4. The role of savings and assets of the aged can easily be overestimated. Use of savings to meet living expenses has a small impact on incomes except for a very small number of the aged. Furthermore, with respect to the major shock of old age, death of a spouse, the assets (and insurance holdings) of couples are generally inadequate for more than meeting the immediate costs of death and the relocation of the surviving spouse. The one important form of asset holding is the (typical) ownership of a house that is paid for. This is important—but the previous conclusion about frequently inadequate receipts was made after full consideration of the fact that receipt requirements are reduced by home ownership.

Operating Guides for Further Research

To what "theoretical formulations or tentative principles . . ." do these facts lead?

The basic stereotype of too much of the thinking about the aged problem is of the somewhat bitter old man who has been forced into involuntary retirement by "mere" age, thus depriving society of potential production, and depriving the individual of income, of purpose, of happiness itself. Such persons exist but they do not constitute the typical aged problem.

Let us face the facts. If we need stereotypes, let us choose the proper ones:

(1) The aged widow, who last worked in 1910 (or 1925), and who has an annual income of perhaps $200 per year. She lives with her son and his family, and only the youngest grandchildren like it.

(2) The aged couple, the husband no longer well enough to work, preserving their household on (if they are relatively lucky) an income of $80 a month (from Social Security, Public Assistance, or contributions from their children). Their savings consist of their house and a paid up life insurance policy of $1000.

But these are only a beginning; more than stereotypes are needed. As a first operating guide it is essential to recognize that while the "aged" are not a homogeneous group, there are several important subgroups that are both large and typically in a tenuous economic position.[6] Chief among them, in order of importance, are those who are victims of the following sources of economic distress: widowhood, illness, and obsolescence of their skills. More attention must be paid—much more—to economic problems other than those of finding employment opportunities for workers who have passed their sixty-fifth birthday.

The problem of the aged woman is perhaps overstated right now, for the last several decades have witnessed an increasingly active degree of labor force participation by

[6] For most problems the appropriate unit of analysis is the couple or the unrelated individual—rather than the family or the individual. In this connection the practice of designating the age of family by the age of "head" in Census tabulations may be highly misleading where the family head is sixty-five or over. Frequently, especially for females, the title is honorific. Our data shed light on this problem, and it is discussed in our full report.

women who, when aged, will be better equipped to cope with the financial problems they face. If this is the direction of solution, there is still much to be done, and the problem must be attacked in terms of encouraging working and finding employment opportunities for women (and wives) in their thirties, forties, and fifties. The motive would be primarily to provide a form of insurance against age rather than merely to augment family income. If a society of career women is not regarded with complete equanimity, our daughters should be advised either to marry men several years their junior or pay more attention to "survivors" provisions of our private and public pension plans.

The solution of the problems arising because of poor health is not an area where the California studies can shed light. This is left hopefully to our medical colleagues. The growth of interest in geriatrics is most encouraging, though one may often wonder whether medical advances will not serve to postpone rather than relieve the disabling effects of degenerative diseases.

Obsolescence of skills is a social cost of the generally applauded social virtue of progress. Certainly attention must be devoted to mitigating this obsolescence, but whether it can be really overcome is one of the unanswered questions that will be discussed briefly in the next section of this chapter.

These problems will repay research. But attention must be directed to broad issues that appear only remotely connected with the aged. Notwithstanding the progress that can be made, it is evident that to a large extent the economic problems of the aged will be mitigated only by the comprehensiveness and generosity of programs of public support of one form or another. The question of form is much less important than the issues of substance.

It is a delusion to place too much hope on getting people once aged to help themselves. This should not discourage the fine efforts that are made: they, however, simply do not form the whole of the problem, nor even the core of it.

Significant Unanswered Questions

Finally, there are numerous questions to which we wish there were answers. Let me suggest a few:

(1) What will be, and what has been, the effect of the remarkable growth of public and private pension programs on the incentives of persons to accumulate savings and assets for their old age? It has been noted already that for the present aged, private accumulation has made small impact. In a sense, the present aged are victims of recent economic history; years of low income in depression, followed by a large and pervasive inflation, have frequently led actual savings to be far below the anticipated levels. Other things being equal, a future generation of aged would be better off. But other things are seldom equal, and we may wonder whether present programs—the principal one is called Social Security—are lulling the future aged into a feeling of false security, or whether by making the problem of private saving the modest and manageable one of supplementing a small though basic income, they will encourage it.

(2) Just how important will be the increased labor force participation of women, which has been a dominant feature of the social scene in the last fifteen or twenty years, when currently young and middle-aged women are themselves over sixty-five. Put differently, must a woman stay continuously in the work force to qualify for employment after sixty-five or to qualify for additional pension rights, or to accumulate sufficient additional savings, or

are periodic forays sufficient? If the latter, what is the minimum requirement?

(3) Is the obsolescence of skills, one source of difficulty of the present aged, a continuing and inevitable feature of our society or a particular one largely confined to the present aged? M. W. Reder, of Stanford University, has suggested that the problem is transitory.[7] He notes that the present aged averaged (median) about eight years of schooling whereas today youngsters average about twelve years. Since education and income appear positively associated, will not future generations, he asks, be better off? In a similar vein he might have argued (but did not) that the chief cause of obsolescence was the shift away from agriculture over the period during which the present aged grew up. Will not every generation find itself, with respect to *some* characteristics, behind the times, and seriously unequipped because of them?

(4) To what extent do the problems of the aged vary importantly for different racial groups? To what extent do they vary regionally? To what extent are they common nationally? Potentially these seem the most important subsumed principles of classification, but perhaps there are others as well.

(5) If the basic economic problem of the aged—poverty —is solved, what will be the impact of the aged population upon the structural characteristics of our economy? What kinds of goods will the aged demand, what sort of housing is appropriate, what differences in savings can be identified for different age groups? Originally, our study hoped to answer these questions, but we found them premature. Nevertheless, these are compelling questions to consider

[7] See Melvin W. Reder, "Age and Income," *Amer. Economic Rev.*, May, 1954, especially pp. 669–70.

as we move toward an aged population that is able to exert an appreciable economic force in our markets. It will be some time before these questions become pressing; much work must yet be done on the more pedestrian—but no less compelling—problems of today.

EMPLOYMENT OUTLOOKS
FOR OLDER WORKERS *Chapter VII*

SEYMOUR L. WOLFBEIN

Seymour L. Wolfbein, Ph.D., is chief, Division of Manpower and Employment Statistics of the Bureau of Labor Statistics. He is also professorial lecturer in statistics, Graduate Faculty, at the American University in Washington, D.C. In 1955 he received the Distinguished Service Award, U.S. Department of Labor. In addition to various articles in technical journals, he is the author of Decline of a Cotton Textile City *and* Our World of Work.

GAUGING THE OUTLOOK for employment for older men and women involves an assessment of practically every substantive matter under discussion, for the prognosis on the employment side depends a great deal on the diagnosis made by our experts on such varying matters as population trends, income maintenance, health and rehabilitation, etc. In order to break into the circle at some point, however, I shall begin with an area where we have been doing some basic research and developmental studies—the work life and retirement patterns emerging in this country.

A Half Century of Change in Structure of Working Life

Because our work in this field has been discussed extensively elsewhere [1] and is relatively well known, I will limit myself to a brief recapitulation of the most important and relevant trends:

[1] Seymour L. Wolfbein, "The Changing Length of Working Life," *Proceedings, Industrial Relations Research Assn.*, December, 1954.

1. As we all know, there has been a tremendous improvement in mortality experience in the United States—so much so that under 1950 mortality conditions, one-third of an initial cohort of baby boys born alive are still alive at age sixty to sixty-four; more than one out of every five are still alive at age seventy to seventy-four.

2. Fifty years ago there was very little difference between total life span and working life among men; for most workers there was no sharp break from employment into retirement as we know it now. Exits from the labor force today, however, have a quite different and distinctive pattern. Among men, for example, the retirement rate today more than doubles between fifty-five to fifty-nine and sixty to sixty-four years of age and reaches its peak in the age groups sixty-five to sixty-nine years. This concentration of retirements during the sixties has become an institutionalized feature of our economy, tied to prevailing conventional retirement plans, both private and public.

3. Increasing life expectancy coupled with the institutionalization of labor force exits has, of course, increased the years of life spent in retirement. Actually, the average amount of years spent by men in retirement has doubled between 1900 and 1950, and our current trends point toward a tripling of this figure between 1900 and 2000.

4. We may recall at this point that equally significant developments have been occurring at the other end of the age scale. There is a very marked and significant increase in the age at which young men make their first full-time entry into the labor force. At 1950 levels, the average American male makes his first full-time entry into the labor force between his eighteenth and nineteenth year of life. At the turn of the century more than one out of every five youths ten to fifteen years of age were already workers (Fig. 1).

STATIONARY POPULATION AND LABOR FORCE

NUMBER LIVING, OF 100,000 BORN ALIVE ANNUALLY

WHITE MALES 1900 & 1950

LABOR FORCE

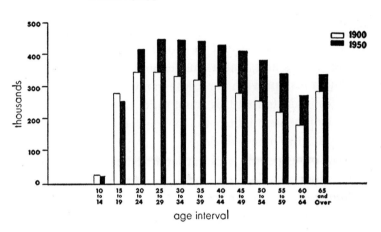

POPULATION

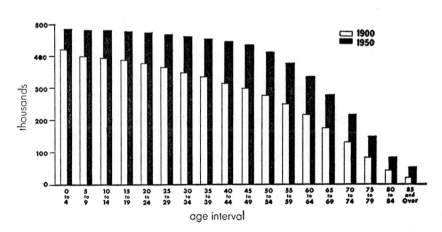

FIG. 1

Now, this double-edged trend has meant a reduction in the number of years of working life at the beginning (later entry into the labor force) and similar reductions at the end (earlier retirement) during the first half of this century. The point is therefore often made that with protracted periods of education and training during youth and higher rates of retirement in older age, more and more of our years are being spent in "nonproductive" or "noneconomic" status and that a smaller and smaller population group must provide for these nonworker activities. Our studies indicate that this is not quite the case. In fact, these developments might better be viewed as follows:

a. Despite the marked delay in entry into working status by young people and earlier exits from the labor force by older people, *men today put in more years of work than did their counterparts 50 years ago.* Further, despite more years of labor force activity, men today spend more of their lives in retirement than did their 1900 counterparts—the answer to this seeming parodox being the added years of total life we have today.

A few figures will illustrate:

Under 1900 conditions

	Years
Man's average life expectancy at birth was	48.2
His work life expectancy was	32.1
And he spent outside the labor force an average of	16.1

Under 1950 conditions

	Years
Man's average life expectancy at birth was	65.5
His work life expectancy was	41.9
And he spent outside the labor force an average of	23.6

b. At least two points should be made in this connection:

(1) In the first place, men today put in a decade more of work during their lives than did their 1900 counterparts. In fact, the manpower potential of a group of 100,000 men living and working under 1950 conditions is hundreds of thousands of man-years more than a similar group operating under 1900 conditions.

(2) It should also be evident from the few figures cited above that men today really spend no greater proportion of their lives outside the labor force than they did in 1900; the longer life afforded them permits both more time as workers and more time for education and training at one end of the age scale and more retirement time at the other.

In this connection, I would also like to add parenthetically that these many added years of working life cannot be consummated unless the older person remains in good health. We will be talking later on about "Health in the Middle and Later Years," "Rehabilitation in Later Maturity," etc. These are particularly pertinent factors in the employment outlook for older persons, and I would like to reiterate what I recently said, viz.: "—the manpower expert knows very well that attrition from the American labor force occurs not only because of death but also because of disability. The disabling effects of chronic illness represent a major threat to the consummation of the added work potential of trends in life expectancy and labor force. . . . Programs looking toward the prevention and control of chronic illness and the rehabilitation of the disabled will therefore make a very direct contribution not only to the general and economic well-being of the individual and his community, but to the national security as well." [2]

[2] Seymour L. Wolfbein, "New Patterns of Planning in a Changing Scene," New Jersey State Department of Health, *Public Health News*, April 1955. Proceedings of Governor's Conference on New Horizons in Chronic Illness Control.

Recent Labor Force Changes

Against this long-term background, we have also been making some search into shorter range changes in the working life of men and have found this to be true: that the ebb and flow of working life in the shorter run appears to correspond very closely to alterations in the general level of economic activity—especially as they are reflected in changing employment opportunities. This is illustrated by our abridged tables of working life. Sharp change in economic climate between 1940 and 1947, for example, reversed long-term trends: age of entry into labor force went down; age of exit went up and these combined to increase the years of working life. Yet, by 1950 when the employment situation changed again, worker rates fell for both young and old; and we had a return to the secular trend of later entry into and earlier exit from the labor force (Table IV).

All in all, a review of the trends of the past decade or so certainly seems to re-affirm the experience of the past half century—especially a very persistent continuation of the downward movement in labor market participation of older men. While men in such age groups as forty-five to fifty-four years and even fifty-five to sixty-four years have pretty much retained their levels of labor market participation, quite the opposite is true for men sixty-five years of age and over. As can be seen from Table III, in 1940, after ten years of depression, the worker rate for men sixty-five and over stood at a little over 44 per cent. As we have already indicated, labor force participation among these men increased considerably during World War II. At the war's peak, their rate was up to 51 per cent —a very sizeable and significant increase. Since the end of the war, however, the rate declined until it reached the unprecedented low level of 39.5 per cent in 1954. In a period of ten years, the labor force rate for men fell a full ten percentage points.

The story for women is, of course, quite different. Women, in fact, have been for quite some time the major suppliers of additional manpower in this country. Among older women the story is briefly this: women forty-five to fifty-four years of age have shown a very significant increase in labor market participation, from a rate of 24.1 per cent in 1940 to 40.8 per cent in 1954; for women fifty-five to sixty-four years there was also a marked upward trend from 18.3 per cent in 1940 to 29.7 per cent in 1954. Women sixty-five years and over participate in the labor force in small numbers only; but here, too, this rate has moved up slightly over the years (Table III).

Recent Employment and Unemployment Trends

The close association between the trends among older persons and the general level of economic activity already alluded to can be seen even more clearly when we assess current developments on the employment and unemployment side. Certainly, the record of the post World War II period in general, and the events of the past few years in particular, underscore again the critical and pivotal importance of the over-all level of economic activity as an overriding factor in determining the employment and unemployment experience of older persons. This record emphasizes the obvious but frequently overlooked principle that there is really nothing quite as propitious for advancing programs and policies in this field for older persons as high levels of economic activity and correspondingly high levels of employment. With a few important exceptions, these high levels have been characteristic of our country throughout the past decade; and they go a long way toward explaining the following developments which, for the sake of brevity, are stated somewhat starkly, with the accompaniment of a few tables for documentation.

1. Older workers have experienced unemployment rates which compare quite favorably with those of other age groups (Table I).

   a. The evidence of the past five years clearly shows no evidence of a disadvantageous differential rate of unemployment among older workers. For each of the months March, 1950 to March, 1955 the unemployment rate among persons forty-five to sixty-four years of age was actually below the average for all age groups; for those sixty-five and over the rate was actually below the over-all average for half the time and only slightly above the rest of the time. In both March, 1950 and March, 1954, months of comparatively high unemployment, persons sixty-five years and over experienced the lowest unemployment rates of any of the broad age groups.

   b. The trend in unemployment among the different age groups between March, 1953 when unemployment was relatively low and March, 1954 when unemployment was at its peak for recent years is quite instructive. During this year the over-all unemployment rate more than doubled for all workers (from 2.7 per cent to 5.8 per cent); but the increase in unemployment rate was lowest for the age group forty-five years and over, and among these, was lowest for the age group sixty-five and over.

   c. Thus, the evidence seems to point to the fact that,

Table I

UNEMPLOYMENT RATES AND PER CENT DISTRIBUTION BY AGE AND DURATION OF UNEMPLOYMENT, SELECTED MONTHS, 1950-55

Age	Unemp. rate	MARCH 1950 Under 5 weeks	5-14 weeks	15 weeks and over	Unemp. rate	MARCH 1951 Under 5 weeks	5-14 weeks	15 weeks and over	Unemp. rate	MARCH 1952 Under 5 weeks	5-14 weeks	15 weeks and over
Both Sexes												
14 and over......	6.7	29.8	41.8	28.4	3.4	45.2	33.5	21.3	2.9	48.8	34.4	16.9
14-19	12.6	35.2	40.4	24.4	7.3	52.2	35.0	13.1	7.7	53.4	32.9	13.7
20-24	9.7	31.9	40.2	27.9	4.4	49.5	34.8	15.4	4.3	57.3	34.7	8.1
25-44	5.8	31.7	42.2	26.1	3.0	48.5	30.9	20.5	2.2	47.4	38.4	14.2
45+	5.7	23.8	42.8	33.4	3.0	36.0	35.3	28.7	2.6	44.2	30.6	25.2
45-64	5.7	24.6	43.2	32.3	2.8	39.5	33.9	26.6	2.5	45.4	31.3	23.3
65+	5.4	18.9	40.2	40.9	4.8	23.3	40.4	36.3	3.2	37.8	26.7	35.6

Age	Unemp. rate	MARCH 1953 Under 5 weeks	5-14 weeks	15 weeks and over	Unemp. rate	MARCH 1954 Under 5 weeks	5-14 weeks	15 weeks and over	Unemp. rate	MARCH 1955 Under 5 weeks	5-14 weeks	15 weeks and over
Both Sexes												
14 and over......	2.7	48.5	34.8	16.7	5.8	34.9	38.0	27.1	5.0	30.4	36.2	33.4
14-19	5.8	49.2	38.9	11.9	11.3	36.2	42.4	22.2	10.2	39.2	36.0	23.8
20-24	4.4	56.6	32.0	11.5	10.3	35.1	40.0	24.9	7.3	40.6	36.3	23.7
25-44	2.1	57.2	30.0	12.8	5.1	37.7	37.0	25.3	4.6	28.2	37.8	33.8
45+	2.4	34.8	39.5	25.7	4.7	29.9	37.3	33.2	4.1	25.3	34.2	40.7
45-54	2.3	35.7	38.7	25.7	4.7	30.4	36.4	33.6	4.0	24.9	34.4	40.9
65+	2.8	30.4	43.5	26.1	4.8	26.5	43.0	30.5	4.3	28.1	33.1	39.6

SOURCE: U. S. Bureau of the Census.

at least during relatively persistent periods of high level economic activity, older persons who remain in the labor force (and we should remember that this was a period of declining worker rates for older men) fare rather well—better apparently than many of the younger folk who, in terms of career development, skills, experience, seniority, etc., experience significantly higher unemployment rates.

2. Upon becoming unemployed, older workers have had more difficulty in getting back to employment (Table I).

    The evidence of the past half dozen years appears to continue to point to the conclusion that older workers do experience relatively higher durations of unemployment than their younger counterparts. This has been true for the entire period since 1950, and has particularly been true during 1954 when unemployment reached high levels in this country. The average duration of joblessness among men sixty-five and over, for example, was about fifteen weeks in 1954—half again as large as that for younger men. The situation may not be as unequivocal, however, as the above statement indicates. Certainly, part of the lower duration of unemployment among the younger people is due to their more frequent job shifting or even to the fact that many of them may not be full-time labor force members but only temporary workers during the school year or during vacations.

3. Older persons have just about maintained their share of available jobs in the United States (Table II).

    a. Between March, 1950 and March, 1955 the total number of jobs in the United States increased by about three million (and it may be added, two out

Table II

TOTAL EMPLOYMENT, BY AGE AND SEX
MARCH 1950, 1953, 1954, AND 1955

Age and Sex	Per Cent Distribution			
	March 1950	March 1953	March 1954	March 1955
Both Sexes				
14 and over......	100.0	100.0	100.0	100.0
14–24	17.9	15.2	14.5	14.1
14–19	6.6	6.7	6.5	5.8
20–24	11.3	8.5	8.0	8.3
25–44	46.3	47.6	47.9	47.5
45+	35.9	37.2	37.5	38.4
45–64	30.8	32.1	32.5	33.4
65+	5.0	5.2	5.0	5.1
Male				
14 and over......	100.0	100.0	100.0	100.0
14–24	15.7	12.5	11.8	11.8
14–19	5.7	5.7	5.4	5.1
20–24	10.0	6.8	6.4	6.7
25–44	46.8	48.3	48.7	48.7
45+	37.5	39.2	39.5	39.5
45–64	31.7	33.3	33.7	33.9
65+	5.8	5.9	5.8	5.6
Female				
14 and over......	100.0	100.0	100.0	100.0
14–24	23.1	21.1	20.6	19.4
14–19	8.7	8.8	8.9	7.5
20–24	14.5	12.3	11.8	11.8
25–44	44.9	46.0	46.3	44.7
45+	31.9	32.9	33.1	35.9
45–64	28.7	29.5	29.8	32.1
65+	3.2	3.4	3.3	3.8

SOURCE: U. S. Bureau of the Census.

of every three of these jobs were filled by women rather than men). Persons forty-five years and over accounted for about 36 per cent of all employment in March, 1950 and about 38 per cent in March,

1955. Among these, the oldest age groups (sixty-five plus) maintained their share of the total by constituting 5 per cent of total employment in March, 1950 and 5.1 per cent in March, 1955.

b. Actually, however, the older worker maintained his position only because of the confluence of two sets of events: on the one hand has been the decline in worker rates already discussed; on the other hand has been the changing population profile among persons of labor force age (fourteen years and older) with higher relative increases in population among older persons. Thus, if we take persons sixty-five and over, labor market participation rates fell from 44.7 per cent to 39.5 per cent between 1950 and 1954—a significant decline. During the same time, however, the population in that age group went up from about 11½ to 14 millions and thus accounted for almost 12 per cent of the population of labor force age instead of about 10 per cent. The increase in population just about counterbalanced the decline in worker rates. We might therefore be justified in heading this section: "Older persons lost in their share of jobs relative to their numbers in the population."

In summary, then, we may say that under rather consistently high levels of economic activity, older workers have not been at a disadvantage in terms of unemployment rates, although they have had relatively more difficulty getting jobs after experiencing disemployment. Their worker rates have continued to decline, however, and only the increase in their numbers enabled them to account for approximately the same share of the increased employment total of the present decade.

Table III

WORKER RATES, BY AGE GROUP, ANNUAL AVERAGES
1940–1954
MALE

Year	Age							
	14 and over	14–19	20 -24	25–34	35–44	45–54	55–64	65 and over
1940	82.6	43.8	95.1	96.6	96.9	93.8	85.5	44.2
1943	87.3	64.6	94.2	98.3	96.4	97.7	88.8	49.5
1944	88.3	69.1	97.1	96.2	99.1	97.7	87.7	50.9
1945	86.7	64.1	94.2	95.2	97.3	97.4	87.1	50.8
1946	82.5	53.3	80.9	95.2	93.4	96.2	86.3	47.4
1947	83.2	53.6	83.7	94.5	96.7	94.1	88.2	46.8
1948	83.3	53.9	84.5	94.5	96.4	94.2	88.0	45.7
1949	83.2	52.9	86.5	94.5	96.5	94.0	86.2	45.9
1950	83.2	52.5	87.9	94.9	96.2	94.3	85.6	44.7
1951	83.6	53.1	89.8	95.8	96.2	94.4	85.9	43.9
1952	83.4	51.3	90.8	96.3	96.5	94.7	86.2	41.6
1953	83.0	50.2	91.0	96.3	96.9	95.1	86.3	40.4
1954	82.7	48.6	90.4	96.2	96.9	95.1	87.0	39.5
FEMALE								
1940	27.9	23.1	49.1	35.1	28.7	24.1	18.3	7.2
1943	35.8	41.4	52.3	38.4	40.9	32.8	24.1	9.8
1944	36.5	41.7	54.7	37.6	41.7	35.6	25.0	9.6
1945	35.9	39.7	53.9	37.7	40.7	35.0	26.1	9.3
1946	31.1	32.1	46.2	32.4	36.4	31.7	22.8	8.3
1947	30.8	31.4	44.7	31.8	36.1	32.4	24.1	8.0
1948	31.7	32.4	45.2	33.1	36.7	34.7	24.0	9.0
1949	32.1	32.2	44.9	33.3	37.8	35.6	25.0	9.4
1950	32.8	31.3	45.9	33.8	38.8	37.6	26.8	9.5
1951	33.6	31.8	46.4	35.2	39.5	39.3	27.4	8.7
1952	33.6	31.3	44.6	35.3	40.2	39.8	28.4	9.0
1953	33.3	30.2	44.4	33.9	41.0	40.0	28.8	9.7
1954	33.4	29.5	45.1	34.3	41.0	40.8	29.7	9.1

SOURCE: U. S. Bureau of the Census.

The Outlook

Gauging the outlook for employment among older persons really requires an assessment of what will happen in the other substantive fields. Perhaps the best way to break into the circle again at this point is to follow the guidelines of the past and inquire to what extent we may expect them to continue into the future. One of the prime determining factors in the outlook revolves around the question: Will older men continue to show declines in labor market activity? As one views the consistent and persistent decline in worker rates (down to 39.5 per cent for men sixty-four plus in 1954, as already shown), one is tempted to say that somewhere along the line soon this drop will be halted. (Even by 1950, the worker rate for men sixty-five years and older was already well below that of teen-age boys.) Tempting as this is, there is little or no evidence to warrant such an assumption—especially in view of the rapid and extensive growth of private and public pension-plan coverage.

One group of experts at the Census Bureau made a more reasonable assumption, i.e., that worker rates will go down among older men, but at rather a slow rate—and they quickly ran afoul of current events. In December 1952, the Census Bureau issued the following prognostication of worker rates for men sixty-five and over: [3]

1950	44.7 per cent	1965	39.6 per cent
1955	42.9 per cent	1970	38.0 per cent
1960	41.2 per cent	1975	36.5 per cent

As the reader will recall, the 1954 rate (39.5 per cent) was already below the one forecast for 1965!

If one therefore goes along with the assumption that worker rates will continue to decline for a while among older men, we come up against the following conclusions:

---

[3] Bureau of Census, "A Projected Growth of the Labor Force in the United States Under Conditions of High Employment: 1950 to 1975," *Current Population Reports, Labor Force* (Washington, D.C., December 10, 1952), Series P-50 No. 42.

a. That the number of older persons in the American working force may very well decline—this in the face of an undoubted increase in their numbers in the population.

b. That we will get, perforce, a significant increase in the number of persons in retirement, a consequent increase in demand for goods and services for retirees, and a consequent underscoring of some of the problems that come with retirement, e.g., income maintenance, health, etc.

c. That, in view of the current and emerging population profile (which involves a minimal number of persons reaching labor force age until the postwar baby crop catches up) and the continuing exodus of older workers, the employment opportunities for those who remain in the labor force ought to be very good indeed. This is especially true if we continue to enjoy high levels of economic activity,[4] and all the more true for older persons if we continue to get growth in such occupational sectors as the professions and white collar jobs where older folk may very well enjoy a competitive advantage.

Some Fruitful Areas of Research

Like all the rest of the associated fields, the general area of labor force employment and unemployment contains many potentially rewarding areas of research. It is impossible to even approach any detailed listing of these in this chapter, so we will confine ourselves to an enumeration of a few of the more significant ones—including those where we hope to be operating in the near future.

1. No one can long work in this field before realizing the great differences in trend and outlook between men

[4] Cf. e.g., 83d Congress, 2d Session, "Potential Economic Growth of the United States During the Next Decade," Joint Committee on the Economic Report, Washington, D.C., 1954.

Table IV

ABRIDGED TABLE OF WORKING LIFE, MALES, 1940,[1] 1947, AND 1950

(1)	(2)	(3)	(4)	(5)	(6)	(7)	(8)	(9)	(10)
	Number living of 100,000 born alive			Accessions to the labor force (per 1,000 in population)	Separations from the labor force (per 1,000 in labor force)			Average number of remaining years of	
	In population	In labor force						Life	Labor force participation
		Number	Per cent of population		Due to all causes	Due to death	Due to retirement		
Age interval									
x to x+n	$\frac{L}{nx}$	$\frac{Lw}{nx}$	$\frac{w}{nx}$	$1000\frac{A}{nx}$	$1000\frac{Q^s}{nx}$	$1000\frac{Q^d}{nx}$	$1000\frac{Q^r}{nx}$	$\overset{o}{e}_x$	$\overset{o}{ew}_x$
	(Within age interval)			(Between successive age intervals)				(At beginning of age interval)	
					1940				
10–14	461,865	6,196	2	431.0	8.2	8.2	—	—	—
15–19	458,100	205,229	44.8	441.6	12.0	12.0	—	51.3	45.8
20–24	452,589	405,067	89.5	68.0	14.9	14.9	—	46.8	41.3
25–29	445,845	429,795	96.4	7.9	17.6	17.6	—	42.4	36.8
30–34	438,014	425,750	97.2	—	28.0	21.9	6.1	38.0	32.3
35–39	428,373	413,808	96.6	—	37.8	29.7	8.1	33.7	28.0
40–44	415,611	398,155	95.8	—	53.3	42.1	11.2	29.6	23.8
45–49	398,028	376,933	94.7	—	80.2	60.8	19.4	25.5	19.8
50–54	373,582	346,684	92.8	—	117.8	85.9	31.9	21.8	16.0
55–59	340,970	305,850	89.7	—	211.6	115.7	95.9	18.3	12.4
60–64	299,545	241,134	80.5	—	376.7	148.9	227.8	15.1	9.2
65–69	248,456	150,316	60.5	—	495.5	191.8	303.7	12.2	6.8
70–74	189,583	75,833	40.0	—	576.4	262.4	314.0	9.6	5.6
75 and over	232,278	44,830	19.3	—	—	—	—	—	—

1947

Age			²						
10–14	475,284	18,320	²	524.1	5.8	5.8	—	—	—
15–19	472,525	259,889	55.0	346.7	9.5	9.5	—	52.6	47.4
20–24	468,041	421,237	90.0	67.2	11.3	11.3	—	48.0	42.8
25–29	462,739	447,931	96.8	6.9	12.6	12.6	—	43.5	38.2
30–34	456,917	445,494	97.5	—	20.7	16.6	4.1	39.0	33.6
35–39	449,323	436,293	97.1	—	32.5	24.4	8.1	34.5	29.1
40–44	438,330	422,112	96.3	—	47.9	36.7	11.2	30.2	24.8
45–49	422,149	401,886	95.2	—	75.6	56.3	19.3	26.0	20.7
50–54	398,186	371,508	93.3	—	106.7	82.1	24.6	22.1	16.9
55–59	365,102	331,878	90.9	—	160.5	115.1	45.4	18.6	13.2
60–64	322,102	278,618	86.5	—	354.7	148.6	206.1	15.3	9.7
65–69	267,931	179,782	67.1	—	501.8	189.2	312.6	12.4	7.0
70–74	204,978	89,575	43.7	—	544.3	258.8	285.5	9.9	5.9
75 and over	263,826	60,944	23.1	—	—	—	—	—	—

1950

Age			²						
10–14	477,806	21,000	²	483.5	5.3	5.3	—	—	—
15–19	475,282	251,899	53.0	354.0	8.5	8.5	—	53.6	47.9
20–24	471,255	418,003	88.7	73.3	9.8	9.8	—	48.9	43.2
25–29	466,652	448,453	96.1	6.0	10.7	10.7	—	44.4	38.6
30–34	461,671	446,436	96.7	—	15.1	14.1	1.0	39.8	34.0
35–39	455,169	439,693	96.6	—	23.3	21.3	2.0	35.2	29.3
40–44	445,488	429,450	96.4	—	42.6	33.4	9.2	30.8	24.9
45–49	430,539	411,165	95.5	—	70.9	51.5	19.4	26.6	20.6
50–54	408,140	382,019	93.6	—	116.3	77.4	38.9	22.6	16.6
55–59	375,956	337,608	89.8	—	195.5	109.7	85.8	19.0	13.0
60–64	332,858	271,612	81.6	—	337.2	142.3	194.9	15.7	9.7
65–69	279,537	180,022	64.4	—	485.9	180.1	305.8	12.7	7.2
70–74	217,261	92,553	42.6	—	558.6	247.5	311.1	10.1	5.9
75 and over	287,742	61,289	21.3	—	—	—	—	—	—

1 Labor force data for 1940 have been adjusted to allow for a revision in Census Bureau enumeration procedures introduced in July 1945.

2 In accordance with current Census definitions, only persons 14 years of age or over are enumerated in the labor force. No meaningful percentage of the population in the labor force could therefore be computed for the age interval 10–14 years.

Prepared by: U.S. Department of Labor, Bureau of Labor Statistics, Division of Manpower and Employment Statistics, November 19, 1954.

and women. Much greater perception can be gained by searching below the over-all data for significant and meaningful differentials in working activity between the sexes among older persons. The National Manpower Council is doing a great deal of work in assessing the underlying features of work as an activity among women; we in the Bureau of Labor Statistics are now in the process of developing companion materials to our Labor Force Life Tables for men which should yield significant information on the structure of working life among women, differentiated by marital status.

2. As we have already noted, even during periods of high level economic activity, we have unemployed older workers—and workers with comparatively high durations of unemployment. Why do these workers, among all others and during good times, experience long-duration unemployment? Are they confined to certain areas, certain occupations, certain general backgrounds of work experience, certain mobility or lack of mobility, certain educational attainment? We hope to make a start in this direction during the next fiscal year in our studies of the characteristics of the unemployed.

3. Whether employed or unemployed, whether contemplating exit from the labor force or remaining in work status, older persons need guidance and counseling on the vocational front. We hope to begin the development of guidance and counseling devices and the formulation of occupational outlook information—all structured for use by older persons.

4. Recent and projected technological development forecasts important changes in the occupational and industrial distribution of employment and important changes in the demand and supply of skills to meet them. Continuing research is needed to assess these developments, espe-

cially in relation to actual performance at various skill levels of older people. We hope to begin exploratory work along these lines during the coming year.

5. Finally, all of us have a stake in performing and supporting all activities which look toward continuing high levels of economic activity. Only through satisfactory levels of economic growth and stability can we hope to achieve really lasting success in our goals for the aging.

AGING AND
RURAL LIFE *Chapter VIII*

WALTER C. MC KAIN, JR.

*Walter C. McKain, Jr., Ph.D., is professor of sociol-
ogy in the Department of Rural Sociology at the
University of Connecticut. He was formerly a social
science analyst with the Bureau of Agricultural Economics of the U.S. Department of Agriculture. His
publications include* Old Age and Retirement in
Connecticut *and numerous articles on rural sociology.*

THE DIFFERENCES existing between rural and urban living
in the United States have become considerably dimmed
during the last half-century. There has been a flow of
urban ideas, urban values, urban techniques, and urban
people into the rural countryside. Not many years ago
communities were widely scattered along the rural-urban
continuum. Today these same communities are more
clustered and fall much nearer the urban extreme. The
rural-urban dichotomy, once a useful distinction in social
research, no longer affords the basic frame of reference.[1]

The two ways of life have been drawn so closely together that any imputed difference between them deserves
careful scrutiny and reappraisal. One area of difference
concerns the adjustment of older people. Many popular
writers and perhaps a few social scientists have given us a

[1] Neal Gross, "Sociological Variation in Contemporary Rural
Life," *Rural Sociology*, September 1948, pp. 256–73.

picture of the idyllic bliss that allegedly accompanies aging in rural America. They point out the simplicity and serenity of rural living. They suggest that older people who have the good fortune to live on a farm or in a small country village can remain usefully and gainfully employed long after their urban counterparts have been discarded. The warmth of friendship, the tranquillity that accompanies sympathy and understanding, and the security of family and rural neighbors are contrasted with the chill of impersonal contacts, the turmoil of the busy city streets, and the insecurity of perpetual change.[2] The time has come to examine these assertions and to test their validity.

Some of the research recently completed in Connecticut gives a tentative and partial set of answers to this question. The research was designed for a different purpose, but the data have been rearranged to focus on the hypothesis that the patterns of adjustment for older people in rural areas do not differ markedly from those of older people in a city environment. The data are restricted to Connecticut, which is basically an urban state. Generalizations must be avoided until similar research can be completed in some of the more rural states. If urbanizing influences, however, continue to pervade rural America, Connecticut may now be in the vanguard of a situation that someday will be typical of rural areas elsewhere in the United States.

Three rural communities and one city were examined. The rural towns were, (1) East Haddam,[3] a rural resort area with some agriculture and a large influx of older people; (2) Scotland-Hampton,[4] two agricultural communities with

[2] Walter C. McKain, Jr., "Should You Retire to the Country," *Journal of Living*, July 1952.

[3] Walter C. McKain, Jr., and Elmer D. Baldwin, *Old Age and Retirement in Rural Connecticut, 1. East Haddam: A Summer Resort Community*. Storrs Agr. Exp. Sta. Bull. 278, June 1951.

[4] Walter C. McKain, Jr., unpublished ms.

farming activity and some in-migration of older residents; and (3) Sprague,[4] a rural manufacturing town with relatively little farming and only slight in-migration. Although all of these communities contained some farming, none was predominantly agricultural. Information concerning the adjustments of all persons sixty-five and over was obtained for each of these communities. There were sixty-three men sixty-five years of age and over in East Haddam; twenty-four in Scotland-Hampton; and seventy-one in Sprague.

The urban community was Meriden, a manufacturing city with a population of 44,000.[5] Meriden was selected as a representative Connecticut city for a research project authorized by the Connecticut Commission on the Potentials of the Aging. One-third of the men sixty-five and over and some of the women in this age group were interviewed. There were 395 men sixty-five to seventy-four years of age who were interviewed in Meriden.

The continued employment of persons beyond age sixty-five is a situation commonly attributed to rural areas. There is ample evidence that farm operators, like other self-employed persons, on the average tend to remain in the labor force for a longer period of time. They can reduce the size of their operations as they grow older, although this practice becomes increasingly uneconomic as agriculture becomes more commercialized, more specialized, and involves a larger investment. Also, they can reduce their own participation in the farm business, either by delegating the tasks requiring arduous physical labor or by sharing the responsibilities of management. Rural

[4] Walter C. McKain, Jr., unpublished ms.
[5] Report of the Connecticut Commission on the Potentials of the Aging. December, 1954.

Connecticut is not confined, however, to farm occupations and not all farmers postpone retirement indefinitely.

Very little difference exists between the rural and urban areas of Connecticut in the number of men sixty-five to seventy-four years of age who are employed (Table I).

Table I

PERCENTAGES OF MEN 65–74 YEARS OF AGE
BY EMPLOYMENT STATUS
Selected Areas in Connecticut

Place		*Total*	*Employed*	*Not Employed*
East Haddam	(1950)	100	47	53
Scotland-Hampton	(1952)	100	48	52
Sprague	(1952)	100	46	54
Meriden	(1954)	100	50	50

One-half of the men in this age group in Meriden were still working. Not quite one-half of the men in the three rural communities were working. Each of the rural communities, with perhaps the exception of Sprague, contained some men who had moved to the area after retirement. Retirement rates in these rural areas might have been much lower otherwise. In Sprague a declining textile industry may have hastened retirement, particularly for men with substantial Old-Age and Survivors Insurance entitlements.

The attitudes toward retirement did not vary much between the farm population and the urban population. In a survey [6] made of 452 commercial farm operators through-

[6] Walter C. McKain, Jr., Elmer D. Baldwin, and Louis J. Ducoff. *Old Age and Retirement in Rural Connecticut, 2: Economic Security of Farm Operators and Farm Laborers.* Storrs Agr. Exp. Sta. Bull. 299, June 1953, p. 36.

out the state, 11 per cent of the farmers in the age group fifty-five to sixty-four indicated that they expected to retire and 25 per cent were uncertain regarding their retirement plans. In the city of Meriden,[7] 24 per cent of the men fifty-five to sixty-four expected to retire. Less than one-fourth of the men approaching retirement age expected to retire either voluntarily or involuntarily.

There was considerable variation in the sources of income of retired men between those living in some of the rural areas of Connecticut and those who lived in the city (Table II).

Table II

PERCENTAGES OF MEN 65–74 YEARS OF AGE
BY MAJOR SOURCE OF INCOME
Selected Areas in Connecticut

Place		Current Earnings	OASI	Savings, pensions	Other
East Haddam	(1950)*	42	9	18	31
Scotland-Hampton	(1952)	50	4	38	8
Sprague	(1952)	43	39	14	4
Meriden	(1954)	43	36	16	5

* Includes men and women 65–74 years of age.

The major sources of income of men sixty-five to seventy-four years of age were similar for the rural town of Sprague and the city of Meriden. Sprague is largely populated by persons who are engaged in occupations covered by the federal Old-Age and Survivors Insurance program. The other two rural areas had a much lower proportion of men who were depending upon Old-Age and Survivors Insurance. Farm operators were not covered by

[7] Report of the Connecticut Commission on the Potentials of the Aging, December, 1954, p. 53.

Old-Age and Survivors Insurance until the 1954 amendments to the Social Security Act.

The persistence of filial responsibility in rural areas is indicated in Table III. The proportion of the men sixty-five to seventy-four years of age who are living with their

Table III

PERCENTAGES OF MEN 65–74 YEARS OF AGE
BY LIVING ARRANGEMENTS
Selected Areas in Connecticut

Place		Total	Living with children	Not living with children
East Haddam	(1950)*	100	28	72
Scotland-Hampton	(1952)	100	38	62
Sprague	(1952)	100	35	65
Meriden	(1954)	100	22	78

* Includes men and women 65–74 years of age.

children is higher in each of the rural areas than in the city of Meriden.

Only 6 per cent of the farm operators of all ages indicated a desire to spend their retirement years with their children.[8] In Meriden, 12 per cent of the men sixty-five to seventy-four years of age expected to live with their children upon retirement. The difference in family solidarity between urban and rural areas still exists but the differential is less than might be expected.

The security that accompanies home ownership is often considered to be a rural phenomenon. Approximately two-thirds of the Meriden men sixty-five to seventy-four years old own their homes. In two rural areas examined, home

[8] Walter C. McKain, Jr., Elmer D. Baldwin, and Louis J. Ducoff. *Old Age and Retirement in Rural Connecticut, 2: Economic Security of Farm Operators and Farm Laborers,* Storrs Agr. Exp. Sta. Bull. 299, June 1953, p. 39.

ownership for this group of men was somewhat higher than in Meriden, but in the third, a smaller proportion of the older men could claim home ownership (Table IV).

Table IV

PERCENTAGES OF MEN 65–74 YEARS OF AGE
BY HOME OWNERSHIP
Selected Areas in Connecticut

Place		Total	Own home	Do not own home
East Haddam	(1950)*	100	69	31
Scotland-Hampton	(1952)	100	88	12
Sprague	(1952)	100	59	41
Meriden	(1954)	100	68	32

* Includes men and women 65–74 years of age.

Although the evidence is scanty, the differences to be found in the rural and in the urban areas of Connecticut with respect to the adjustments made by older persons do not support the commonly held belief that older people in rural areas differ markedly from their urban cousins in (1) their employment status after age sixty-five, (2) their acceptance of retirement as a way of life, (3) their major source of income, (4) their living arrangements, or (5) their tenure status.

The pastoral fantasy that glorifies the rural community as a paradise on earth for older people may not be verifiable but it is none the less convincing for an increasing number of retired people. Each year many older persons are moving to the rural areas of Connecticut. Some have retired from urban industry and are seeking an escape from the complicated and somewhat bewildering city life. Others are lost without something to do. They hope to find a way to be useful in a rural setting. They harbor the belief that they can adjust to the slow and easy pace of rural activity and continue to make a contribution to society. The quest for financial independence also draws some older people to rural areas. Part-time farming and subsistence agriculture are looked upon as methods by which limited incomes can be stretched.

The older people who move to rural Connecticut are a diverse lot, and their problems of adjustment as well as their effect on the rural communities in which they settle are varied. One group consists of the wealthy urbanites who purchase farms and finance their operations with non-farm income. Very little is known about these so-called "hobby farmers" and their effect on rural communities. They are frequently condemned by local people as unfair competition, since they can outbid their less fortunate neighbors for labor, machinery, and land. They are self-supporting, however; they add to the tax base, and they can afford to experiment with new and untested farm management techniques.

Some of the older people who move to rural areas are persons who are seeking to make a livelihood in agriculture. Many in this group are doomed to disappointment and they are looked upon as a potential burden by rural communities. There is some evidence that the turnover in this group is large. Many of them return to the city.

The largest group of older persons who migrate to rural areas are persons who do not expect to enter the labor force. In some instances they purchase farm properties and use them as rural residences. Since economic forces apparently call for a decline in the number of farm units, the in-migration of older persons and other suburbanites may be fortunate. Most rural people, however, look with some alarm at this changing pattern of land use.

The retired worker, buffeted about by the perplexities

of urban life, his services no longer in demand, and his budget threatened by the high cost of urban living, seeks understanding, a sense of usefulness, and perhaps a new source of income in a rural environment. There has been a rapid urbanization of rural America; urban ways and attitudes have penetrated most rural communities. The friendly, neighborly, "gemeinschaft" life has not been replaced completely; but many aspects of rural living have become as impersonal, as calculated, and as contractual as life in the city. Agriculture itself has become increasingly commercialized and large outlays of capital are required in almost any farm enterprise. Mechanization and specialization on the modern farm also act as barriers to the entrance of newcomers.

Actually very little research has been undertaken in the field of aging and rural life. Most of the statements appearing above are conjecture based on scant information. Descriptive research is needed in many rural communities before the more analytical research avenues can be charted effectively. There are a number of questions, however, that could well be investigated at the present time. A listing of some of these follows:

Socio-economic factors affecting the consumption of specified agricultural products by older persons. The estimated increase in the number of persons who will be sixty-five years of age and older suggests that they will constitute an important market for various agricultural products. When their present consumption habits are charted and compared with the habits of other age groups, estimates regarding the need for farm products can be made. Any gap between actual consumption and the intake called for by nutritional standards can be noted and related to such factors as retirement status, income, family setting, marketing procedures, ethnic groups, and many others.

The potential contributions of older persons in rural areas.   It has been suggested that there is a vast reservoir of human resources to be found among the older population living in rural areas, particularly, among those people who have recently moved from urban centers. Many specialized services, both governmental and voluntary, do not require full-time employment in the more sparsely settled areas. Rural librarians, nurses, assessors, caretakers, civil defense administrators, and many other rural persons work on a part-time basis at low salaries. Older persons may be ideally suited for this kind of work, but only a few communities have effectively utilized their services.

Retirement preparation in rural occupations.   The extension of Old-Age and Survivors Insurance to farm operators and laborers may have changed the retirement plans of farm workers. The effect of this upon their plans for economic security should be noted. In addition, an analysis of individual preparation and guidance for retirement by farm organizations and agencies should be examined. Experience among urban workers suggests that financial security is not sufficient to guarantee adjustment in old age.

The effect of the migration of older persons upon land use in rural areas.   The removal of farm land from agricultural use, zoning, taxation, and the provision of services are among the topics of concern to rural areas in which there has been an in-migration of retired persons.

Social participation of older persons in rural areas.   Transportation problems, poor health, the absence of special-purpose groups (such as Golden Age Clubs) probably reduce both the formal and informal social participation of older persons. Information is needed on the ways in which this situation can be remedied. In addition, the substitutes for these activities, such as radio and television programs, should be analyzed.

Expansion of proposed research projects. By including a rural sample in proposed research in other fields, differences that may exist between rural and urban living for older people can be noted.

HEALTH IN MIDDLE
AND LATER YEARS *Chapter IX*

CECIL G. SHEPS

Cecil G. Sheps, M.D., is executive director, Beth Israel Hospital, Boston, and lecturer on Preventive Medicine, Harvard Medical School.

IN THE FOLLOWING CHAPTER, the basic physiological, pathological, and clinical aspects of the primary health problems of old people will be outlined, after which there will be presented the principles and problems involved in developing the health services required to bring the benefits of medical and social science to the aged.

The Aging Process

Aging and disease are different processes. From the biological point of view aging is a natural condition. It starts before birth at the moment of conception and goes on throughout life.

Aging is a complex continuous biologic phenomenon which affects all living organisms and is related to the passage of time. At any point in time it is the resultant of two antagonistic and compensating processes of growth and atrophy or involution. Atrophy and destruction occur even in embryonic life and during the dramatic and spectacular growth period of childhood and youth, but are, of course, greatly outstripped during this stage of the life of an individual. With the passage of time, a point is reached at which the balance between continuous growth and atrophy tips in favor of the latter.

These processes of growth, atrophy, and replacement are highly differentiated. They vary greatly depending upon the specific cells, organ, or body function concerned. For example, the life span of cells varies from that of three to four days for certain formed elements of the blood to sixty to seventy years or more for some cells of the nervous system.

There are great differences between individuals in the rate of aging. For example, it has been found that some persons aged eighty have renal function as good as the average for the forty-year group. Almost any type of measurement for aging will produce similar findings. Chronological age, we see, differs markedly from biologic age and cannot be used as an indicator of functional capacity. Biologic aging is, therefore, a highly variable personal and individualized process.

There is also a wide variation in the rates of aging in the same person. In each individual it is a process with involution, decreased adaptability, and loss of reserve capacity appearing in one organ system sooner than in others. Thus, rather than being a uniform deterioration, the rate of aging varies in different parts of the body in asymmetrical fashion. No individual is of the same biologic age throughout. A person may have a cardiovascular system equivalent to the average of forty-year olds and a digestive system characteristic of sixty-five-year olds.

The peak or optimum effectiveness of all human physical and mental functions is not reached at one and the same time. The "prime of life," even in the purely physical sense, is reached at widely different ages depending upon the nature of the activity. The age at which records are broken for short sprints is between eighteen and twenty-two years, whereas for marathons, the champions are often between thirty-eight and forty-five years old. There are compensations which follow upon the changes of age. For example, as muscular vigor and speed decrease, co-ordinating skills often increase.

The question, "How old is this person?" cannot be answered in any single unit or dimension. It must be restated to read, "How old is this person with respect to a specific functional capacity or a series of such specific functions?" Multiple measurements are thus needed to determine where the balance of capacities of a particular individual place him on the continuum which represents the human organism's inexorable journey from conception to death.

We do not, of course, know to what extent the changes of aging are due to the inherited constitution of the individual, as distinguished from the vicissitudes, insults, accidents, stresses, and strains of living. From the research point of view, it is very difficult indeed to separate out the influence of environmental factors. At a recent working seminar at Chapel Hill, North Carolina, on "Needed Research in Health Care" a group of medical and social scientists adopted a general statement which contained the following:

Many diseases, including most of those which are now of greatest importance in terms of numbers of victims, have some kind of relationship to age. Age and the diseases which often appear in older people are not the same thing or a single complex. Age must be studied as an independent variable if the roles of time and continued risk and exposure are to be understood in either a purely scientific or a purely practical sense. Research programs should be adjusted to this end and studies of the fundamental processes of ageing itself, and their relation to disease development, need enlarged and long-continuing support. Long-term, multidisciplinary studies are needed to answer vital questions about the ageing process—questions that range from the dynamics of cell structure and function to the problems of adaptability under different psycho-social circumstances.[1]

Another interesting and pertinent series of questions requiring intensive study concerns the problems of optimum levels. We know what the average level of the pigment hemoglobin is in the blood of humans in the Western World. We know average weight for age and sex. But what is the optimum or best level for these elements and indicators?

The general biologic characteristics of the aging process include a slowing down of cell and tissue activity and response as shown through a wide range from gradual tissue desiccation, retardation of cell division, and tissue oxidation to decreased strength of skeletal muscle and impaired vision and hearing. A striking resultant is the decline in the ability of the body to adjust to emergencies,—a decline in the safety factors, the homeostatic mechanisms which balance such vital body constants as body temperature, water, concentration of sugar, proteins, and electrolytes in the blood.

The intensity of symptoms is therefore greatly reduced in old people, making it necessary to evaluate seemingly minor and subtle changes; thus greater diagnostic skill in the treatment of older people is required. Aging reduces the tolerance of some people to drugs, and increases that of others. Nutritional needs also change. There is, for example, a reduction in caloric requirements but an increased need for calcium and protein.

There are also changes in the function of organ systems. The separation of factors due to age from those due to

[1] Cecil G. Sheps and Eugene H. Taylor, *Needed Research in Health and Medical Care* (Chapel Hill: University of North Carolina Press, 1952), pp. 12–13.

disease is still very difficult in the cardiovascular system. In the digestive system changes in volume and chemistry of various digestive juices are recognized. Many changes, of course, take place in the endocrine system. Alterations in the skin and skeletal system are also known although, as with the others, there is still much to learn about the underlying mechanisms and processes.

The aging of our population is the general descriptive term used to signify the fact that we now have a much greater proportion of our population which is over the age of sixty-five and the outlook is that this proportion will continue to increase. Of the three factors responsible for this, virtual cessation of immigration, reduction in the birth rate, and improved survival, an examination of longevity or survival expectancy will be helpful in pointing up the general characteristics of the problems of older people so far as health and sickness are concerned.[2]

In 1900 the expectancy of life at birth in this country was fifty years. Now it is about seventy, an increase of twenty years. For the average person who is now sixty-five, the expectation of life is barely two years more than it was in 1900. Thus old people are not living to be much older, but rather many more people are living to be old. This is due primarily to the victories over acute infectious diseases. In 1900 the five leading causes of death were, in this order, pneumonia, tuberculosis, diarrhea, heart disease, and kidney disease. Now they are heart disease, cancer, deaths by violence, apoplexy, and kidney disease. Between 1900 and 1920 the reduction in the incidence of typhoid, tuberculosis, diphtheria, diarrhea, and enteritis alone corresponded to a saving of 230,000 lives each year in the United States. With more people living to the middle and later years, with the acute communicable dis-

[2] See Chapter IV for a discussion of these factors.

eases being better controlled, the importance of chronic diseases looms greater than ever.

The Rise of Chronic Illness

In 1900, chronic illness was responsible for approximately half the deaths. Now it is responsible for 60 per cent of all disability and for 80 per cent of the deaths. Thus, more than three-fourths of the deaths today are terminal events from long-standing chronic illness.

Old age and waning capacities must be distinguished from disease. There is no disease so specific as to be found only in the aged. Though acute illness with relatively rapid recovery is more characteristic at younger ages, it is not confined to the young. Similarly, the chronic diseases which are progressive or from which recovery is slow, though more characteristic of the older ages, may be found at all ages. As a matter of fact most of the chronic diseases of later life have their start in middle life. It is the deaths that occur later. Fully one-half of those who are chronically ill are below forty-five years of age, and more than three-fourths are in the age period fifteen to sixty-four years.

The group of diseases that we are discussing are usually called "degenerative diseases." Stieglitz [3] offers a more descriptive and probably more accurate phrase, "chronic progressive disorders of later life." These disorders fall into five major groups: circulatory disorders, metabolic disorders, cancer, the arthritides, and the nervous system and sensorium.

A simplified classification (after Stieglitz) of the more

[3] E. J. Stieglitz, "The Relation of Gerontology to Clinical Medicine," in *Problems of Aging, Transactions of the 12th Conf.* (N. Y.: Josiah Macy, Jr., Foundation, 1950).

important diseases showing the more pertinent relationships follows:

A. Circulatory disorders
   1. Chronic infective myocardial disease
     (a) Rheumatic
     (b) Syphilitic
   2. Hypertensive arterial disease
   3. Arteriosclerosis
     (a) Cerebral: apoplexy

               dementia
     (b) Coronary: cardiac disease
     (c) Renal: chronic nephritis
   4. Combination forms
B. Metabolic disorders
   1. Diabetes mellitus
   2. Anemia
   3. Climacteric; female and male
   4. Gout
C. Malignant tumors, all forms
D. Arthritides
E. Nervous system and sensorium
     (a) Deafness
     (b) Cataracts
     (c) Paralysis agitans

By and large, there are very striking differences between most of the diseases characteristic of maturity and old age and those disorders that are most commonly found in youth.

The causation of disease in youth is usually fairly obvious, exogenous, specific, single, and of recent occurrence. The etiology of diseases of later life, on the contrary, is usually obscure, endogenous, multiple, cumulative, and distant in time of occurrence. This makes specific prevention of the occurrence of many of these diseases difficult, at present. In youth the onset and symptoms are violent, obvious, and often immediately distressing and even severe. In the later years, it is most often insidious, mild, and indirect, often existing and progressing for a long period of time without any disability or symptom complaints. The disease is often considerably advanced before symptoms occur, thus making for delay in discovery and diagnosis. In youth, the course of disease is usually acute, self-limited, brief, immunizing, with little individual variation. In senescence, the cause is usually chronic rather than immunizing; it often produces increased vulnerability to other diseases. It is progressive and there is very wide individual variation. This produces long-lasting disability prior to death.

The difficulties inherent in any approach to the complex problems of chronic disease in general, and in older people in particular, call for imagination, flexibility, and a great deal of basic and applied research. The health gains we have made in this country in the past 50 years have placed the United States in a position of leadership among the countries of the world. We do, however, lag behind some countries in some fields. A comparison of the United States with seventeen other countries, recently made by Dublin and Spiegelman,[4] shows that while we lead in eliminating child and adolescent mortality, we are not so successful toward the later years of life. As a matter of fact, we are particularly bad in combatting the so-called degenerative diseases among males over the age of forty-five, and also accidents among both sexes.

We must, of course, continue to press forward with basic research into the pathology and treatment of the chronic diseases. As has been pointed out, "Great progress is being made in discovering heart disease and in managing

[4] L. I. Dublin and M. Spiegelman, "Factors in the Higher Mortality of Our Older Age Groups," *Amer. Journ. P. H.*, 42: 4 (1952).

cardiac patients so as to make their condition more bearable and so as to delay total disability and death. Real advances in understanding the mechanics of healthy and diseased hearts and blood vessels are continuing and merit every support. But there is far too little research on the whole man—his individual physiology and its reaction to the way he lives his life—in relation to his future cardiac health or disease. *Before* heart disease is discoverable, individuals can differ in their mode of life and in every morphological, biochemical, physiological, and social characteristic we can measure. It is reasonable to expect that these individual differences in the healthy state are related to the great differences in the eventual appearance of or freedom from heart disease. . . . Prevention must be the keynote and the hope, but so far there is extremely little to offer because almost nothing is known of the pre-disease personal characteristics, of the life-long habits, of the factors of diet, of exercise, of emotion, of physical and social environment, of other illnesses and accidents far removed in time, which make one man a candidate for early death and give his fellow man relative immunity." [5]

Prevention and Treatment

In thinking about the etiology of disease, it is helpful, particularly in relation to chronic diseases, not to confine oneself to single specific pathogenic agents alone. There is often much useful merit in thinking about predisposing causes, precipitating causes, and prolonging causes. A good illustration of this is the data which has fairly recently become available on the relationship between obesity and deaths from cardiovasculo-renal disease and diabetes.

[5] Sheps and Taylor, *op. cit.*, p. 11.

Evidence exists also that a reduction in weight, after a period of being overweight, reduces the mortality rate to a level comparable with those of average weight.

From the point of view of health services, the attack on chronic illness must take place on two broad fronts. One is prevention and the other is adequate care and rehabilitation. For the drama of difficult diagnosis and the danger of acute illness we must substitute emphasis on prevention, on limitation of disability, and on the fullest restoration of residual capacities. This calls for radical change in the attitudes of the public, and also of the medical profession.

Prevention can be thought of as primary and secondary. Primary prevention means averting the occurrence of the disease; this can be applied effectively, for example, to certain types of heart disease such as rheumatic and syphilitic, to tuberculosis, and to certain types of cancer.

Secondary prevention is an approach of great potential value. By this we mean the stopping of the progression of a disease from its early unrecognized phase to a more severe one, and the preventing of complications and disability. This involves screening procedures applied to whole populations, groups en masse, or to selected portions of the practice of a private medical practitioner. The detection of diseases in these early phases requires the application of screening tests, examinations, and diagnostic procedures. This approach has value in relation to such diseases as, for example, cancer, cardiovasculo-renal disease, visual and hearing defects, diabetes, and tuberculosis.

Medical and social progress has in the past few decades produced many new types of professional and technical personnel and new types of institutions. It is no wonder that, with new medicine and with new problems, new methods of service should be developed. We have acute general hospitals, chronic disease hospitals, convalescent hospitals, custodial institutions, homes for the incurable, homes for the aged. The past decade has seen the development of multiphase screening programs, home care, and the emergence of rehabilitation as a vital and crucial function of medical care.

The Commission on Chronic Illness has published a most excellent and comprehensive statement [6] of recommendations for the care of the long-term patient. It is stated at the beginning that care for the chronically ill is inseparable from general medical care, that care and prevention are inseparable, and that rehabilitation is an innate element of adequate care and properly begins with diagnosis. There are sections on the patient at home and in an institution, on coordination and integration, on education and personnel, and on research and financing. This is a horizon-stretching, pace-setting statement of great value.

The medical care which people receive depends, of course, on their use of health personnel and health facilities. Only when patients recognize their needs, and by some payment arrangement seek help, do services become possible.

Three Basic Challenges

Perhaps at the risk of oversimplification I would say that the three primary challenges that face medicine today, particularly with reference to the care of chronic illness, are those represented by the need for making necessary and feasible adjustments to give due recognition in actual practice to the wholeness of man, the need for developing

[6] *Chronic Illness Newsletter* (Commission on Chronic Illness), June, 1955.

the essential unity of health and medical services, and the need to arrange for adequate financing for this program.

The specialization of medicine which has brought us a great many benefits has also fragmented medicine so that we now must knit it together to enable the various types of personnel to function better as a group or team. Continuity of care is a relatively new watchword of the utmost importance. It carries with it implications which extend not only to the various specialties in medicine, but also to the various types of institutions that we now have.

When one tries to obtain satisfactory definitions of the functions of various types of institutions, for example, acute general, chronic, convalescent, aged, incurable, and custodial, one becomes frustrated indeed. What is more, it is soon realized that this approach regiments thinking within the confines of institutional ideas that are now out of date. What is needed is a dynamic approach to the function of various types of institutions and programs, directed at the needs of patients and based upon the individual needs of patients under varying circumstances. This has of course been done in a most striking fashion by Dr. Cosin who, in his program, has with such great effectiveness made a distinction between the frail ambulant patient and the ambulant patient who is in a further stage of convalescence.

A new spirit needs to be infused into our institutions. The acute general hospital is now oriented towards the person who passively accepts care and has things done for him. Active participation of the patient is, of course, essential in the care of patients with chronic illness. The other institutions on the other hand require a more dynamic approach to their activities. In Sean O'Casey's autobiography, *Sunset and Evening Star*, there is a description of an English nursing home where his wife was a patient;

he said, "The rooms were heavy with old air, and wore a weak look, as if they, too, were sick: and all I saw seemed to whisper cynically of uncleanliness and clumsy uncomely methods of management and care." This is a description which is applicable to many institutions in this country, too. Repairing this deficiency is not simply a question of facilities or personnel, it is also a question of attitude and point of view which pervades institutions. There is a very serviceable French aphorism which says, "It is the tone that makes the music."

The problems of financing care for chronic illness and for the aged certainly deserve attention. In spite of the fact that there has been a tremendous increase in the coverage of the population with voluntary health insurance of one kind or another, it was found in 1951 that, while 57 per cent of the whole population had some form of hospital insurance, only 26 per cent of those over sixty-five were similarly protected.

Some Research Needs

There is much research that needs to be done in this general field. At the Chapel Hill seminar it was stated that "there is great need for applied research leading to the development of methods of education and service which will most effectively raise the level of health practices of individuals and communities and increase the quality and availability of health care. It has been amply demonstrated in the field of nutrition, for example, that an alteration of attitude or behavior cannot be brought about without adequate knowledge of the psychological and cultural factors which affect them. Such studies of motivation related to health require the combined methods, concepts, and insights of the biological and social sciences.

"Administrative research in medical care is of the greatest importance now that adequate medical care for all is becoming accepted as a desirable component of our standard of living. There is much to be learned about the best technique for mobilizing community action toward health goals such as the construction of a hospital, or the development of and participation in a group prepayment plan. There are a great many questions in the general field of medical care requiring answers. Among them is the need for developing reliable means of evaluating community health resources such as personnel, physical facilities, and existing community services. The value of a medical care program depends on the degree to which it assures early diagnosis and prompt and thorough treatment at the least expense compatible with high standards of service. Every facet of existing programs must, therefore, be objectively and carefully studied and experiments must be conducted so that we may evolve methods of giving service and providing payment which are based on established facts relating to the above criteria." [7]

In closing, it must be recognized that it has been possible to touch only the top of the waves in the vast sea of health and research problems. One is here reminded of the words of Alfred North Whitehead, who said, "Here we are with our finite beings and physical senses in the presence of a universe whose possibilities are infinite, and even though we may not apprehend that, these infinite possibilities are actualities."

[7] Sheps and Taylor, *op. cit.*, pp. 13–14.

MENTAL HEALTH IN
ADVANCED MATURITY   *Chapter X*

EWALD W. BUSSE

*Ewald W. Busse, M.D., is professor of psychiatry
and chairman of the Department of Psychiatry at
Duke University, Durham, North Carolina. From
1946 to 1953, he was professor and head of Psycho-
somatic Medicine at the University of Colorado. He
is also a Diplomate in Psychiatry, and is certified in
Clinical Electroencephalography.*

THE MENTAL and emotional changes that frequently accompany old age have been recorded since the beginning
of medical observation. The etiology of such changes and
the possibility of reversibility have received little attention. Until a few years ago most physicians were content
to attribute these changes either to arteriosclerotic brain
disease or to so-called senile dementia. Competent investigators have demonstrated, however, that either of the
two clinical diagnoses is often not confirmed by post-
mortem gross and microscopic examination of the brain.
This immediately forces us to consider the first question:
"What other explanations for these psychic changes are
possible?"

Among the most recent publications which deal with
the mental health of elderly people is the report called,
"The Aged and Aging in Illinois" by Drs. Bettag, Slight,

Weining, and Sorenson.[1] These investigators present statistics which indicate that the proportion of elderly persons being admitted to state mental hospitals is increasing twice as rapidly as the proportion of the general population admitted. The increasing proportion of the aged requiring hospitalization because of so-called mental illness raises a second question: "Why is an increased proportion of our aged population unable to remain adjusted to the community?"

Studies in the Processes of Aging

In an attempt to answer, at least in part, the questions raised above, my colleagues and I initiated an extensive investigation of elderly people. Using a multidisciplinary approach, we have studied some of the psychological and physiological changes which appear in old age; we have attempted to evaluate the interrelationships, particularly the effects upon the central nervous system.

The number of subjects we have studied to date exceeds 500. These subjects have been separated into various groups which were determined both by social and economic status and medical condition. Sixty years of age was arbitrarily established as the lower age limit for our subjects. No upper age limit was set. The routine for each subject included the following: (1) detailed social and medical history; (2) blood and urine studies, determination of NPN and fasting blood sugar; (3) physical and neurological examination; (4) psychiatric examination; (5) electroencephalograms; (6) psychological testing, which included a Rorschach, Wechsler Adult Intelligence Scale,

[1] "Part I—The Mentally Ill," *Research Study* 68–1, *Illinois Department of Public Welfare* (Springfield, Ill., 1954). This investigation was supported by a research grant from the National Institute of Mental Health of the National Institutes of Health, United States Public Health Service.

and in some instances the Weigal Color Form Sorting Test, the Level of Aspiration Task, and the Successive Eight Test. Other procedures carried out on specific subjects include determination of Flicker Fusion Frequency for light, photographs of the retina of the eye, and direct microscopic observations of the capillary blood flow and the bulbar conjunctiva.

Our study was initiated several years ago in Denver, Colorado, but has now been shifted to Duke University in Durham, North Carolina. This makes possible the comparison of cultural factors upon the aging population. Although it is evident that there are some cultural influences which are of import, our studies are as yet incomplete in this area, and we will have to delay our discussion on this particular problem until a later date.

As previously mentioned, the subjects were divided into various groups on the basis of specific criteria. For the purpose of this presentation, we shall limit our discussion to those groups referred to as "community groups," and one hospitalized group. All the elderly persons in the community group were considered to be making an adequate social adjustment and were initially believed to be free of any disease which directly involved the central nervous system. Any disease recognized prior to the inclusion of a subject in our study was considered to be minimal for the subject's age. Those placed in the community group A were unemployed, considered to be indigent or semi-indigent, and were recruited as volunteers from the facilities of a university clinic. This group includes one hundred subjects—fifty-two women and forty-eight men. The average age was 70.9 years.

Community group B was made up of persons who were retired but making a satisfactory adjustment in the community. They were all of higher financial status than those placed in group A. The number of persons in the community B group was fifty. However, all the data presented are not necessarily based on the complete group. The smallest number of subjects in the community B group, utilized for statistical purposes, was thirty. The average age was seventy-two years.

The C group was the smallest and included forty subjects, all of whom were working, although past the usual age of retirement. Their average age was slightly less than seventy-two years. A small community D subgroup, composed of ten physicians with an average age of seventy-five years, will be briefly referred to. All of them to various extents were continuing their interests and activities in medicine.

The hospitalized senile group was made up of one hundred persons, who had been admitted to a psychiatric unit because of what was believed to be either senile or arteriosclerotic brain changes. The average age in this series was approximately seventy-seven years.

Electroencephalographic Findings

The EEG's have been of interest because of the large number of focal findings which appeared in all of the groups of elderly persons which we have studied.[2] It is necessary to indicate briefly the criteria which were used in determining normality. Some slower waves in the frequency range of 6–8/sec. were allowed as long as the dominant rhythm remained between 8–12/sec. or was of the type usually referred to as low voltage fast activity. Therefore, many records were called normal which in younger adults

[2] E. W. Busse *et al.*, "Factors That Influence the Psyche of Elderly Persons," *Amer. Journ. Psychiat.*, 110 (1954): 897. See also A. J. Silverman, E. W. Busse, and R. H. Barnes, "Electroencephalographic Findings in 400 Elderly Subjects," *EEG Clin. Neurophysiol.*, 7 (1955): 67.

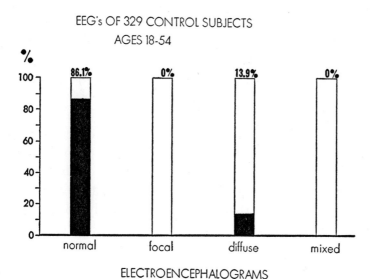

EEG's OF 329 CONTROL SUBJECTS
AGES 18-54

FIG. 1

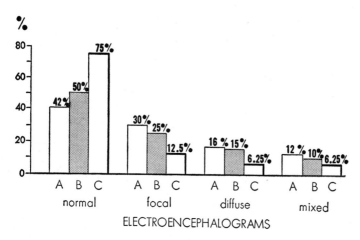

COMPARISON OF EEG FINDINGS IN COMMUNITY
GROUPS   Ä   'B'   'C'

FIG. 2

would be considered to be mildly slow. Only those records were called diffusely abnormal in which the frequency spectrum appeared to be definitely shifted.

Before reviewing the findings in our subjects, let us look at the results found in a control group of 329 normal adults ranging in age from eighteen to fifty-four years. Some 86 per cent of this control group had normal brain waves; 14 per cent showed mild disturbances, and there were no focal abnormalities (Fig. 1). This control group should be contrasted first with the findings in the community A group. Here we found that only 42 per cent had normal EEG's; 30 per cent had focal changes; 16 per cent diffuse slowing; and 12 per cent were found to have both diffuse and focal abnormalities. It is at once apparent that with advancing age there has developed a marked change in the physiological functioning of the brain. The most striking change is the appearance of localized abnormalities.

In all of the various groups studied, 75 per cent of these foci were located in the temporal areas and of these, eight out of ten were found in the left anterior temporal region. Ten per cent were in the right temporal area and the remaining 10 per cent appeared alternately or synchronously in both temporal leads. Further consideration will be given later to the high percentage of left temporal foci. Although focal abnormalities are also present in community groups B and C, it must be noted that there is a definite increase in the percentage of normal records in these groups. Group B contains 50 per cent normal records and group C has 75 per cent (Fig. 2). The decrease in the percentage of focal records should also be noted. These findings seem to indicate that those individuals who continue to work in spite of the fact that they are beyond the usual age of retirement have a more normal functioning brain as measured by the EEG. The possibility that this is significant is given support if the community groups are contrasted with the senile or hospital group. When elderly people are incapable of adjusting in their environment and must be placed in a psychiatric institution, 30 per cent have normal EEG's, diffuse abnormalities and mixed abnormalities predominate, while the number of pure focal records is only 14 per cent.

Although it would seem likely that a focal disturbance in these elderly persons would in some way affect their psychological functioning, the manner in which it does so has escaped our observation. We can find no evidence that those with focal disturbance alone have any decrease in their intellectual capacity. In fact, there is questionable evidence that those with temporal foci function better as measured by psychological testing than those with a normal EEG. They were better able to learn new patterns and were more flexible. In a previous report,[3] possible Rorschach differences were explored with an emphasis upon possible impairment of perceptual clarity by determining the F+ percentage. Here again there was no evident difference in perceptual clarity between subjects with just focal disturbances and those with normal EEG's. When the subjects have diffuse brain wave slowing or a mixed type of dysrhythmia, however, the many obvious changes in their mental functioning give evidence of organic brain disease. To return to a further discussion of the significance of the preponderance of left temporal abnormalities, one would be justified in speculating that the slowing is related to cerebral dominance. At the present time, however, we do not feel justified in making a

[3] L. L. Frost *et al.*, "Rorschach Findings as Correlated with Physiological Changes of the Aging Process," *Journ. Gerontol.*, 7 (1952): 479.

statement regarding its possible correlation with cerebral dominance, since all of our patients with right temporal foci were right-handed, and the few left-handed individuals in the study with focal abnormality had foci in the left temporal area. A possibility that the EEG changes could be correlated with evidence of cardiovascular disease also occurred to us, but there again we were unable to detect any consistency between the status of the cardiovascular system and the focal changes of the EEG.

Emotional Changes and Responses

It is not possible to report upon all areas of our investigation.[4] We have explored and already reported our findings in regard to marital and sexual adjustment, the relationships of our elderly subjects to their children, their religious beliefs and activities, their habits in regard to work, planned creative activity and recreational activity, frequency of recurrent periods of depression and other things, such as constipation, insomnia, and so on.

Some of the conclusions reached from those studies include the following: (a) A poor relationship between old people and their children is part of a life pattern of neurotic and immature behavior. (b) Psychologically, elderly persons who continue to work beyond the usual age of retirement have a higher intellectual capacity than those who do not. (c) Guilt is not an important psychic determinant in elderly persons and is not the major cause of feelings of depression. Depression is more often related to

---

[4] A. J. Silverman *et al.*, "Physiologic Influences in Psychic Functioning in Elderly People," *Geriatrics*, 8 (1953): 370. See also E. W. Busse *et al.*, "The Strengths and Weaknesses of Psychic Functioning in the Aged," *Amer. Journ. Psychiat.*, 111 (1955): 897. See also E. W. Busse, R. H. Barnes, and A. J. Silverman, "Behavior Patterns in the Aged and Their Relationship to Adjustment," *Dis. Nerv. System*, 5 (1954): 1.

loss of self-esteem because of the feelings of inferiority. (d) Those individuals who were relatively free of depression have certain patterns of behavior and psychic functioning which they utilize as a means of obtaining satisfactory adjustment. Subjects who continue to occupy their time by working have an excellent method of warding off depressive episodes, as do those subjects who engaged in adequately planned creative activities. (e) Successful patterns of adjustment are rarely developed in old age; it is evident that those individuals have participated in planned creative activities for many years.

General Conclusions

Although our studies have resulted in some interesting observations and conclusions, it is evident that a great deal of work must be done before we know why increasing proportions of our aged population require hospitalization in mental institutions. Society has produced numerous stresses which make it harder for the individual to maintain a level of functioning which is acceptable to the community. The criteria of what is acceptable behavior has also become more rigid, and it is clear that society in many respects must become more understanding of elderly persons.

Extensive investigation is needed and undoubtedly will be carried out so that we can more fully understand the physiological and pathological changes found in elderly people.

RELATIONSHIP OF AGE AND MENTAL TEST SCORES AMONG OLDER PERSONS *Chapter XI*

GEORGE K. BENNETT

George K. Bennett, Ph.D., is president of The Psychological Corporation. He is a Fellow of the New York Academy of Sciences and is the author of several psychological tests as well as numerous articles in professional journals. At the present time he is serving as chairman of the Ad Hoc Working Group of the Technical Advisory Panel on Personnel and Training Research to the Assistant Secretary of Defense.

IF ONE ASKS the question of what is known and unknown about the effect of increasing age upon intelligence test scores, one is forced to admit that for the seventh and eighth decades, very little is known. Moreover, in spite of our present ignorance, little research seems currently to be underway.

In an attempt not to overlook any recent work, the index pages of the *Annual Review of Psychology* for the years 1952 to 1955 were scrutinized. In three of these volumes no reference was found to the relationship of age and test performance. In the 1954 issue the work of Vincent and Birren is mentioned. Vincent's article is primarily a summary of what has previously been published and provides no new data. Birren reports a factorial analysis of the

Wechsler-Bellevue Intelligence Scale which touches only incidentally on the effect of aging.

Wechsler, in the third edition of the *Measurement of Adult Intelligence,* published in 1944, summarizes earlier research and arrives at the conclusion that intelligence reaches a peak in the early twenties, thereafter declining at a linear rate. The principal basis for this opinion is Wechsler's analysis of the standardization data from the Wechsler-Bellevue Scale. Wechsler draws many analogies to bodily functions and apparently is somewhat selective in his evaluation of earlier research. The rate of loss, so far as can be estimated from his statement, seems to be about one standard deviation in thirty years, although no numerical indication is given.

As quoted by Carroll in the *Annual Review* for 1954, Vincent finds that, "the decline of mean score on various tests with age can be regarded as practically constant, that this decline operates for both timed and untimed tests, and that the mean annual decline from age twenty-one to sixty is approximately .03 standard deviation." Since Vincent used Wechsler's material as a primary source, it is not surprising that the results are so similar; this cannot be regarded as independent confirmation.

In the course of standardizing the Wechsler Adult Intelligence Scale, which is the revision of the Wechsler-Bellevue Intelligence Scale, an attempt was made to obtain a representative sample of the adult population of the United States. The primary sample consisted of 1,700 cases divided among seven age groups. In each age group men and women were equally represented. Using data from the 1950 United States census, the sample in each age group was selected to be closely proportional to the population at large with respect to geographical region, urban-rural residence, race, occupation, and education. The age groups were 16–17, 18–19, 20–24, 25–34, 35–44, 45–54, and 55–64. In addition, through the cooperation of the Committee on Human Development of the University of Chicago with support from the United States Public Health Service, 475 individuals comprising a random sample of people over sixty years of age residing in the Kansas City area were tested. It is believed that the data from these two samples provide a somewhat better source of information about the relationship of age to test scores than do the data previously available.

The Wechsler Adult Intelligence Scale consists of eleven subtests, six of which contribute to the Verbal Score and the remaining five to the Performance Score. The Full Scale Score is the sum of the verbal and performance portions. The standardization sample is described in the Manual for the Adult Intelligence Scale, while an article by Doppelt and Wallace appearing in the October 1955 issue of *The Journal of Abnormal and Social Psychology* describes the work with the older sample. These recent results do not coincide very closely with Wechsler's earlier analysis or with Vincent's curve.

The figure which has been distributed shows the relationship of the three scores to age and also includes the curves postulated by Vincent. In each case there is a tendency for test performance to attain its peak in early maturity and to decline thereafter. The rate of decline is much slower for the Verbal tests, however, and appreciably slower for the Full Scale Score than we should expect on the basis of the earlier statements. In the case of certain of the subtests, the retention of ability is even more marked. Scores on the vocabulary, information, and comprehension parts of the Wechsler Adult Intelligence Scale are maintained throughout the national sample at about as high a standard for individuals around sixty years old as

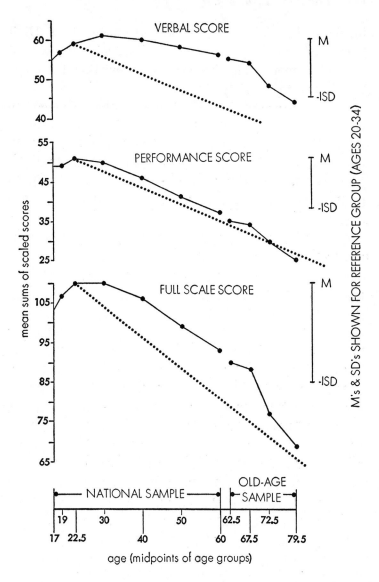

_____ Mean sums of Verbal, Performance, and Full Scale
scores on *WAIS* for age groups in national and old-age
samples.
.... Vincent's formulation.

Fig. 1

for those about nineteen. Of the Performance tests, Digit Symbol shows the most rapid decline, with the loss of somewhat more than one standard deviation from age twenty-two to age sixty.

When we turn to the second sample—those above sixty years of age—the decline is more marked. Moreover, it should be pointed out that these data do not include individuals who were too ill or infirm to complete all eleven subtests. The effect of including them would have been to show an even more rapid decline in the years after sixty-five.

Offsetting this to some degree is the fact that those tests in which the greatest deterioration appears seem to be the ones which call for acuity of vision and manual agility. It is conceivable that as persons grow older, a larger proportion suffer from the lack of proper eyeglasses and that some of the apparent loss may be due not to intellectual but to sensory impairment.

Anyone interested in generalizing from these data is welcome to do so, but some of the hazards should be pointed out. This, like previous studies, is cross-sectional. During the life span of the older persons, the average level of education has increased appreciably, and we are far from certain as to the amount of test score improvement produced by further schooling. Changes in the nature of education have taken place during the same period, and these might operate either to raise or lower test scores.

There seems to be evidence that the retention of verbal skills is markedly better than was anticipated; nevertheless, the progressive decline is amply demonstrated. It seems obvious that the data so far available are woefully inadequate as a basis for any description of the relationship between chronological age and intelligence test performance.

This topic is of such present and future significance that a large-scale, carefully designed study should be undertaken with public funds to produce highly dependable data upon which many aspects of public policy could be based. A study of this sort should be longitudinal in nature so that differences in prior education and cultural environment can be taken into consideration. It should include a variety of physiological and medical tests as well as a far broader sampling of intellectual and manipulative skills. It should cover the age span at least from forty to eighty years. It is obvious that the results will be needed in much less than forty years from the beginning of such an undertaking, but this can be accomplished by having initial samples at each semi-decade with the first follow-up five years hence and a second in ten years. Thus, by a sort of shingling operation we shall be able to span within a comparatively few years a range four or eight times as great.

If we lack such information as would be provided by a study of this nature, decisions directly affecting the lives of older people and more generally affecting the whole American population will be made on a basis of conjecture rather than fact.

References

Birren, J. E., "A Factorial Analysis of the Wechsler-Bellevue Scale Given to an Elderly Population," *Journ. Consulting Psych.*, 16 (1952): 399–405.

Vincent, D. F., "The Linear Relationship between Age and Score of Adults in Intelligence Tests," *Occupational Psych.*, 26 (1952): 243–49.

Wechsler, David, *The Measurement of Adult Intelligence* (3rd ed.; Baltimore: Williams & Wilkins, 1944).

THE OLDER GENERATION
AND THE FAMILY *Chapter XII*

ERNEST W. BURGESS

Ernest W. Burgess, Ph.D., is professor emeritus of sociology, Department of Sociology, University of Chicago. His publications include The Family, *Predicting Success and Failure in Marriage, and co-authorship of* Personal Adjustment in Old Age *and* Introduction to the Science of Sociology. *He has recently completed a study of the sociological aspects of trailer camp retirement villages in Florida.*

THE RELATION of the older generation to its adult married children and to its grandchildren has undergone something like a revolution in the past one hundred years. In the middle of the nineteenth century the grandparents held the central, honored, and authoritative position in the family. The old husband and his wife were the patriarch and the matriarch of the large family group of children, grandchildren, and great-grandchildren.

The rural community of the past provided a favorable environment for the rise and persistence of this extended type of family. The large number of children supplied sons for farm hands and daughters to help the mother with household tasks. Married sons and daughters usually lived in the same neighborhood or at least near by. Sunday was the day of reunion at the old homestead. Visiting within the circle of the extended family was a matter of custom and of duty.

The sons worked for their father until they were twenty-one. As soon as a son married, his father would set him up on one of his farms or help him acquire a farm. Usually he remained more or less economically dependent on his father. The daughter after her marriage still depended for help and advice upon her mother, particularly at the times of childbirth and in the rearing of her children.

The tempo of social change was slow and the cultural differences between generations were small. The extended family tended to be a socially self-sufficient unit. The shift from the agricultural society of the past to an industrialized and mechanized economy undermined the factors making for the solidarity and cohesiveness of the extended family. These factors were: large number of children, economic dependence of adult children (particularly sons on the father), proximity of residence of the older and younger adult generation, prestige in the community of the aging parents, and cultural homogeneity of the members of the extended family.

In the city, especially among the middle classes, a small rather than a large number of children was of economic advantage. Children no longer were an economic asset and, as soon as they could obtain employment, were economically independent. They were also less likely to remain after marriage near the home of their parents. In the city the great majority of older persons were employees rather than self-employed, as on the farm. Upon retirement they lost status and many faced the prospect of economic dependence upon children less able than their rural counterparts to care for them. Even more disruptive of the earlier extended family unity than any or all of these together was the growth of cultural diversity between the older and the younger generation. The aging parents were stigmatized as "old-fashioned" and "mid-Victorian" by their modern and less conventional adult children.

In short, the extended family was falling into the separate pieces of its component small family units. The old system of family relations was disrupted and no new system of relationships had evolved. Yet the expectations and sentiments of the earlier period tended to persist although the situation in which they arose had changed. Older persons still expected services, deference, conformity to their demands and advice, and their adult children in withholding them experienced guilt feeling and remorse.

At present, then, there is confusion and conflict because the relation of the older and the younger generation has not been re-defined in terms of the present situation.

Concretely, specific problems have arisen that call for analysis and consideration. Among these are the following three questions:

1. Should children offer an aging parent or parents a home?

2. What should be the moral and legal responsibility of children for the financial support of indigent parents?

3. What, if any, should be the reciprocal roles of aging parents and their adult married sons and daughters?

The realities of the present situation as existing in the urban way of life are: small size of family, apartment-house living without parlor and guest room, the disappearance of servants, the considerable expense involved in adding a new member to the household, and the growth in cultural diversity and personality differentiation.

Prevalence and Composition of the Three-Generation Family

At the present time a high proportion of older persons are living with their children, rather than alone or with non-relatives. Our figures have not been exact because the census data did not separate children from other relatives. A much more accurate breakdown of the living arrangements of the aging is, however, now provided by the sample census of April 1952, obtained by the United States Census Bureau for the University of California at Berkeley through personal interviews with persons sixty-five and over in about 15,000 households in sixty-eight sample areas located in forty-two states and the District of Columbia.

This survey found that one-half (50.5 per cent) of persons sixty-five and over were married and living with their spouses. Of the older men, two-thirds (67.5 per cent) and of the women, only one-third (35.1 per cent) were married and living with wife or husband. This study for the first time revealed the proportion of older persons residing in the same home with their children, broken down between those where the aging parent was head and those where an adult child was head of the family. Of the households in which older persons lived, just over one-third (35.2 per cent) were three-generation families. These are evenly divided between those in which the aging parent is head and those in which an adult child is head.

Detailed data from this study are presented in Table I by couples, and by males and by females who are widowed, single, divorced, or separated.

The first striking fact evident from these data is that very few older couples (only 3.3 per cent) are living in homes where an adult child is head. On the other hand, seven times as many couples (22.6 per cent) are living in homes where an aging parent is head.

The second outstanding fact revealed by this table is the much higher proportion of females than of males who are widowed, single, divorced, or separated, and living

Table I

LIVING ARRANGEMENTS OF OLDER PEOPLE, 1952
Percentage Distribution

Living or not living with children	Couples	Widowed, Single, Divorced, and Separated	
		Males	Females
Not living with children	74.1%	69.3%	54.7%
Living with children	25.9	30.7	45.3
Older person head	(22.6)	(11.0)	(15.9)
Adult child head	(3.3)	(19.7)	(29.4)
Total	100.0%	100.0%	100.0%

with their children (45.3 per cent and 30.7 per cent).

The third significant fact disclosed by these data is that nearly double the proportion of older persons who are widowed, single, divorced, or separated are living in homes where the adult child is head as where the aged parent is the head (19.7 versus 11.0 per cent for men and 29.4 versus 15.9 per cent for women).

In considering all older men and women together, in regard to their living arrangements, three times as high a proportion of women as of men are living with their children. Fathers much less than mothers are taken into their children's homes. The proportion of mothers to fathers living with their adult children is three to one.

Special studies confirm the finding that many three-generation families result from the mother moving into the married daughter's home,[1] that a majority of living grandparents come from the mother's side of the family, presumably because women marry younger and live longer,[2]

[1] Marvin R. Koller, "Studies of Three-generation Households," *Marriage and Family Living*, 16 (1954): 205–6.

[2] Ruth Albrecht, "Relationships of Older Parents with Their Children," *Marriage and Family Living*, 16 (1954): 132–35.

and that couples maintain closer relations with parents of wives than with parents of husbands.[3]

Two forms of three-generation families have been identified above: (1) those headed by the aging parent and (2) those where the adult child is head. While they present certain similarities, the differences are as important or perhaps more important from the standpoint of human relations. A typical situation of the family headed by an aged parent is where a newly or recently wedded couple takes refuge in the parental home because of a housing shortage or because of insufficient income and/or unemployment. Studies indicate that this type of living arrangement is associated with unhappy marriages of young couples in large part by reason of frustration in not being able to set up independent housekeeping but instead being relegated to a dependent status. The three-generation family headed by the adult child reverses the superordinate-subordinate relation. Here the older person gives up his independent status and is assigned a dependent role with the accompanying loss of status and consequent unhappiness.

Will the Three-Generation Family Survive?

The question of taking an aging parent into the home of a married son or daughter may be viewed first as a matter of free choice on both sides. An example is that of a mother aged seventy whose husband has just died leaving her with a small but adequate income. Shall she reside by herself, move into an old people's home, or go to live with one of her two married children?

[3] William M. Smith, Jr., "Family Plans for Later Years," *Marriage and Family Living*, 16 (1954): 36–40, and Paul Wallin, "Sex Differences in Attitudes to the 'In-law,' a Test of a Theory," *Amer. Journ. Sociol.*, 59 (1954): 466–69.

First, the question may be considered from the stand-point of the daughter and her husband. As modern young people they no longer feel the imperative of the duty to offer the widowed mother a home. Nor do they adhere to the rigid principle that two women cannot live happily in one household. Nor are they concerned with what their friends will think about their decision. They discuss the matter in terms of the housing accommodations that they can offer and whether or not she will fit into their routine of living, promote or impede the development of the grandchildren, share in part their friends and interests, and, to some extent, be able to live her own independent social life. On the basis of these considerations they offer or withhold an invitation.

The widowed mother, who is sensitive to the changed realities in the relations of the generations, does not as-sume that an invitation will be forthcoming. And if it is, she gives it careful consideration. She realizes that, in general, it is likely, on the average, to work out more suc-cessfully if she is to live with her daughter rather than with her son and daughter-in-law. She asks herself whether her daughter and husband have been realistic in appraising the situation of interpersonal relations and the effect of the entrance of a third adult into the family circle. She is also concerned, if she has vital interests and a circle of congenial friends, about her opportunity to live an inde-pendent and satisfying life.

More and more older people of sufficient means are adopting the principle of independent living as, in gen-eral, the right solution to this question. At the same time, they are attempting to work out mutually satisfying rela-tions with their children and grandchildren.

Responsibility of Adult Children

The second question is: what should be the moral and legal responsibility of adult children for the support of their indigent aged parents?

In the rural society of one hundred years ago the moral and legal responsibility of adult children to support their aging parents was unquestioned and afforded real security to older people. The great fear of many an older person, especially if childless, was the dreaded alternative expressed in the saying "over the hill to the poorhouse."

Today the question of legal responsibility has become a matter of sharp controversy. The existence of Old Age Assistance seems to call into question the earlier assumption of universal and complete responsibility of adult children for the support of indigent parents.

Much of the debate hinges on the question of the ability of adult children to support aging parents under modern conditions of urban life. A review of the facts [4] appears to support the following conclusions:

1. The total burden of support of aged parents by children has increased since 1900 due, first, to the quadrupling in the last fifty years of the aging population, and second, to their increased expectancy of life after sixty-five years.

2. The number of adult children of the aged per family has declined, leaving a smaller number to assume support for a given aged parent.

3. Under urban conditions, fewer adult married children have an extra room to house an aged parent, and a move to larger quarters increases family expenditures.

4. In cramped quarters friction between the members of a three-generation household is likely to increase.

[4] See also *The States and Their Older Citizens* (Chicago: Council of State Governments, 1313 E. 60th Street, 1955), pp. 21–24.

5. It costs more to support parents than it did under rural conditions.

6. Children of the aged today have more children of their own with increasing costs for their rearing and education.

Not only the ability of children to support aging parents has declined but the expectation of receiving such assistance has diminished. In the only nationwide survey on this question an average of 89 per cent of 3,515 employees, sixty-three and sixty-four years old, in a sizeable number of establishments answered that they "do not expect to receive any support from members of their families, friends, or anyone else when they stop working." Of these same persons, 42 per cent in the median industrial group stated that "Social Security and a pension from their employers will be their only source of income when they stop working." [5]

A state-wide study of Old Age Assistance recipients in California disclosed that only 29 per cent believed that adult children should be required by law to support their parents.[6]

Income statistics indicate that a considerable proportion of families would find it difficult to support an aging parent without lowering their standard to the point which would make them eligible for public assistance.

Half of the 48 states have met this situation by establishing income scale provisions to determine the ability of adult children to contribute to the support of an aging parent. The base monthly sum which requires support from a son or daughter ranges, before federal income

[5] Cornell University, *The Study of Occupational Retirement, First Progress Report* (Ithaca, 1953), p. 20.

[6] Floyd Bond, *et al., Our Needy Aged* (New York: Henry Holt, 1954), pp. 296–300.

taxes, from $187 for non-urban areas and $238 for specified metropolitan areas in Virginia, to $410 a month in Alabama and Georgia.[7] A comparison of these figures with the income of families and unrelated individuals for 1950 indicates that the great majority of adult children receive incomes below the amount of the legal requirement for support.[8] This law, then, exempts all but a fraction of adult children from this legal responsibility.

Even when children are able to support their parents, as determined by a legal scale of ability, several states report great difficulty in enforcing payments. Action by courts is costly, prosecuting attorneys may be reluctant to act because of political repercussions; delays occur, court decisions may be unfavorable and, if favorable, the orders may be evaded.

Consequently, it is not surprising to find only a small difference in the proportion of persons on Old Age Assistance in states with and without a recovery and lien law designed to prevent older persons from conveying property to their children in order to become eligible for Old Age Assistance.

Other factors, however, besides legal responsibility operate to induce adult children to offer financial support to their parents. These factors range from pressure of community opinion, feelings of moral responsibility and affection, to positive desire to include the parent in the family circle. As a result, approximately as many needy parents are supported by their children as are at present on Old Age Assistance rolls.

[7] Elizabeth Epler, "Old-Age Assistance; Determining Extent of Children's Ability to Support," *Social Security Bull.* 17 (1954): 8.

[8] *Statistical Abstract of the United States 1954* (Washington, D.C., 1954), p. 312.

Changing Reciprocal Roles

There remains the third question: What, if any, should be the reciprocal roles of aging parents and their adult married children?

In the past the reciprocal roles of aging parents and their adult children were well defined and clearly understood. The parents were the transmitters of culture, knowledge, and wisdom; the adult children looked to them for counsel and advice. The parents had supported their children in childhood and youth; it was the duty of the children to support their parents in old age. In short, the parent-superordinate role and the child-subordinate role continued throughout life.

Under urban conditions this rigid type of reciprocal role has broken down and parents and their adult children are striving to establish a new relation adapted to the urban situation.

Many married couples are quick to utilize their parents as baby sitters when they want an evening out. Some fond grandparents are glad to give this service, but the majority resent the role of baby sitter if they sense that they are being exploited and their own plans and interests are being disregarded.

What, then, should be the relation and role of parents and children? It is plain that adult children reject any notion that their parents are guiding their lives. The son does not go to his father about business matters but to an expert. The daughter knows that the way she was brought up by her mother is the wrong way to rear her baby. She turns to the pediatrician and to the latest book by a child psychologist. Often the children find that their interests and activities diverge markedly from those of their parents so that they have less and less in common.

Some grandparents would like, if they could, to re-establish the old-time relation of a century ago, at least in its social aspects. One gentleman in his fifties stated his expectation of a happy old age as follows: "I am planning on buying a country house with enough rooms for all my children, their husbands and wives and grandchildren on their vacations and other visits. They will always know that in times of adversity my home is a haven. I hope to enjoy their respect and confidence."

An older man who had retired said: "I agree with your statement 100 per cent for everybody—except myself. My wife and I have a large country house with three bedrooms and three screened-in sleeping porches. We are always delighted when our married son, his wife and children, and our married daughter and her husband and children come for a visit. But after two days of visiting when they say goodby, how relieved my wife and I feel."

The new relation of parents and adult children needs to be based on the recognition that each generation has its own life to lead. The older generation should give up the expectation that its chief interest in life is to be preoccupied with the affairs of their children. The younger generation should realize that in living their own lives, there still remains an area of common interest with their parents.

A chief problem appears to be that of making the shift from the parent-child relation of childhood and youth to a new relation characteristic of adult persons. One older man in an interview spoke of shifting his role from that of father to friend. Other older people, in discarding the notion of the father as an authority or as an advisor to his son as outmoded, agreed upon the term "a companion" as more in keeping with the times.

In this new relation, what is the reciprocal role of parents and adult children?

The parent still remains the one person to whom adult children can turn with certainty in times of adversity or crisis. If the young husband is unemployed or in business trouble and all other recourse has failed, he knows he can find help and refuge with his father or with his wife's father. When the daughter expects a baby or is ill, she knows she can appeal to her mother and count on her dropping everything else to come to her assistance.

But what can aging parents expect from their children? They can, I think, count in a similar way upon sons and daughters for help in times of economic difficulty and of illness, although perhaps not with equal certainty.

In conclusion, it is evident that, from the standpoint of each generation living its own life, residing together in a three-generation household will not be on the average the best dwelling arrangement. One study found that living independently but relatively near each other seemed to be the optimum situation for the majority of cases.

One area of common interest is unique in intergeneration relations as compared with other human contacts. This area is the body of common experiences that parents and children enjoyed when living together. On both sides there is the desire to revive and continue these. Auspicious occasions are birthdays and holidays. These are and should be celebrated as family occasions.

The communication and association of the two generations will no longer be a matter of routine, custom, and duty. It will rather be spontaneous on both sides and be greater or smaller in relation to the affection, congeniality, and mutual interest of parents and their adult children.

The three questions of the desirability of the three-generation household, moral and legal responsibility, and reciprocal roles of parents and their adult children, have been analyzed in terms of the shift from the old-time rural neighborhood to the industrial city. The answer to all three questions appears to have been the same. The decline of familism and the growth of individualism have reduced the weight of considerations of the law, custom, and duty. At the same time, they have increased the part which affection, congeniality, and common interest play in the relation of the older generation to the family.

PERSONAL AND SOCIAL ADJUSTMENT

IN OLD AGE *Chapter XIII*

ROBERT J. HAVIGHURST

Robert J. Havighurst, Ph.D., is professor of education and chairman, Committee on Human Development, University of Chicago. He was formerly director of the Institute for Problems of Old Age. In 1953–1954 he was Fulbright Professor at Canterbury College in New Zealand. His publications include co-authorship of Personal Adjustment in Old Age, Older People, *and* The Meaning of Work and Retirement.

IN SPEAKING about personal and social adjustment we speak about the goal of human living at any age. There is an inner harmony which is personal adjustment, and a harmony with the world around us which is social adjustment. The problem for a science of gerontology is to understand these harmonies, to describe them objectively, to measure them if possible, and to find out how they are related to each other and to other aspects of human life.

It should be said that the meaning of the term "adjustment" should be obtained from the context in this discussion, and not from some preconceived judgment as to what the word must mean. This word has several possible meanings. It is *not* used here in the sense of conformity to a mediocre or materialistic set of social standards. Instead, it is a state of harmonious living which does not exclude tensions and conflicts with unworthy standards.

In studying adult life and old age, if we would deal with the important things, we cannot avoid such questions as happiness and the goals of life. We want to know what makes people happy and what makes life profitable. We want to know what experiences in earlier years, what conditions of middle age, what social relationships, what achievements, and what attitudes lead to successful old age.

To make a scientific study of these matters we need, above all, a definite, measurable concept of successful living in middle age and old age. With this we can hope to answer some of the many questions that we can now only argue about, such as: what about compulsory retirement, should older people live with their adult children, should older people migrate to warmer climates, should older people in the church be in groups of their own age or in mixed-age groups? Of course there is no simple answer to any of these questions, but we cannot discover the complex answer until we have some way of measuring successful living.

It seems reasonable to identify successful living with some combination of personal and social adjustment. Consequently it is desirable to define and measure personal and social adjustment. When this task is done, the problem of what combination or combinations of personal and social adjustment should be equated to successful living will remain to be solved in one or several ways. It is the former task—the definition and measurement of personal and social adjustment—that we are undertaking at the University of Chicago.

The Definition and Measurement of Social Adjustment

For the definition of social adjustment the concept of social role seems useful. A social role is a complex pattern of behavior which is learned by a person in response to the expectations of others. Social roles may be defined in narrow or broad terms, so that a person's social life may be said to consist of his behavior in as few as ten or as many as a hundred social roles. For this research a rather broad definition of social roles seems to be useful. We can describe at least 95 per cent of an adult's social behavior in terms of the following ten roles: parent, spouse, child of aging parents, home-maker, worker, user of leisure time, church member, club member, friend, and citizen.

These social roles are defined by the social groups in which we live. We say that a man "makes a good father" or a "good husband." We say he is a good worker but an indifferent church member, an active club member but an apathetic citizen. All these evaluative statements mean that we have a concept of the good father, the good husband, worker, church member, etc., against which we measure the actual behavior of people.

As social scientists, we attempt to make explicit these concepts of good performance in the various social roles, and to work out scales for measuring the performance of people in them. Then, by observing and interviewing people we can measure their social role performance. Each person can be given a score on each of ten social roles, or one or two less in case he does not fill certain roles. For a total score his scores in the several role areas can be averaged.

There are many difficulties in this process. Chief among them is the problem of defining successful performance in a given role so that it covers people of both sexes and in various social classes. Since sexes and social classes differ somewhat in their expectations of a good father, worker, home-maker, etc., we may either try for a definition which includes the expectations of the various groups and is "fair" to all of them, or we may set up different definitions for different cultural subgroups. We have tried to do the former. Another difficulty is to define successful performance in a given role in terms of the ideals of society rather than in terms of average practice. Average practice usually falls considerably short of the social ideals. It is not always easy, however, to get general agreement on the nature of the social ideals for the roles of worker, friend, club member, etc. in our kind of society.

There are other difficulties, but our experience is that it is easier to define and measure social role performance, and therefore social adjustment, than it is to define and measure personal adjustment.

Definition and Measurement of Personal Adjustment

For clues to the definition of personal adjustment in adulthood and old age I refer to three papers by Raymond Kuhlen, Robert Peck, and William E. Henry, respectively, presented at the Conference on Psychology of Aging held under the auspices of the Division on Maturity and Old Age of the American Psychological Association.[1] All three make the point that a person to be well adjusted must be able to cope with a complex world. All three deal with personal qualities which enable one to live successfully in a complex world. Some of these qualities are: affective complexity, or variety of emotional reactions to various situations or stresses; tolerance of ambiguity; flexibility; and expansion of emotional and intellectual interests. Opposed to these concepts, and indicative of poor adjustment are: rigidity, simplicity, and constriction.

The importance of being equipped to live in and deal with a complex world may be illustrated by the cases of

[1] John E. Anderson, ed., *Psychological Aspects of Aging* (Washington, D.C.: American Psychological Assn., 1956).

several Mexican grandmothers whom we found in our study of adult life in Kansas City. These women were from Mexican peasant families. They came to Kansas City as young wives with their husbands who got jobs as railroad laborers. Living in the bottoms near the railroad yards they have raised families and are now surrounded with grown children and grandchildren. Typically, such a woman spends her days at home looking after grandchildren, chickens, and a plot of flowers. She attends a Mexican movie once a week, and tunes her radio to a station that broadcasts Mexican music. She goes to church on Sunday, and reads a Mexican weekly newspaper. She enjoys a new stove which her son has given her, and bakes things for her grandchildren to eat. She is not a citizen and therefore does not vote. Her life is a set of simple routines. She has no plans for the future.

These women were mostly quite happy, and we were happy to find such simple people living so happily, but we could not say that they were well equipped for life in Kansas City. Their grown children were more complex persons, probably not so happy, but better equipped to get along in the kind of life they will have to lead in this society. It is true that the grandmothers have an inner harmony, but it is too simple a harmony for this kind of society. The new generation of Mexican-Americans may not be so happy, but they will have a chance to create a more complex inner harmony of needs and interests and emotions. If simplicity is the standard for personal adjustment, the grandmothers have it. If the ability to enjoy a complex of satisfactions and to deal with a complex of stresses is the standard, the new generation has it.

Personal adjustment in our kind of society may be a complex harmony of needs, interests, and emotions, changing to meet the changing situations of life as a person moves through life from adulthood to old age.

If this is taken as a definition of personal adjustment, then some of the observable characteristics may be the following:

(1) *Expansion of emotional and intellectual interests.* After the work career is well established and after children are grown up and on their own, many people fail to find new things to care about and work for. They suffer from constriction of interests. The successful person finds new things to care about in community affairs, adult friendships, and new leisure activities. President Eliot of Harvard wrote to William James when both were about 60, saying, "We have a sense of growth and increased capacity for useful service. We find our lives enriched and amplified from year to year. So long as this enlarging process goes on, we shall be content."

(2) *Flexibility.* After middle age the ordinary person meets a good many difficulties due to the decline of his physical and mental vigor, the loss of loved ones, and the loss of status that come with old age. His reactions to these difficulties may be rigid, unimaginative, stubborn, and over-cautious; or his reactions may be tentative, experimental, and open-minded. If he behaves in the first way, he is "intolerant of ambiguity," to use a phrase of Frenkel-Brunswik. Adult life brings many ambiguous situations, which are both threatening and promising, and where the possibilities are not clear. A person can make them turn out well if he acts flexibly, but he can refuse to tolerate ambiguity by defining situations prematurely or by running away from such situations.

Another way to look at flexibility or tolerance of ambiguity is to examine the nature of a person's *perception of roles available to him.* A person's perception of the roles open to him defines the world of action open to him. If he sees his roles limited to those of worker, citizen, and home-maker, and if he perceives these roles in their most standard, traditional forms, he is likely to have difficulty as he grows older. If, however, he perceives these roles in novel ways, or if he perceives the roles of home-maker, spouse, user of leisure time, church member, club member, and friend as means of satisfaction to him, he will define for himself a satisfactory life.

(3) *Affective complexity.* Henry describes the person characterized by this attribute as one who is sensitive to a variety of experiences. He is able:

to respond to other people and other ideas, different from his own, rather than reacting against them;

to accept differences as natural rather than as a threat;

to utilize his past emotional experience in guiding his own behavior;

to tolerate a certain degree of personal inconsistency in himself.

Henry suggests that either a very high degree or a very low degree of affective complexity will indicate unsuccessful outer adjustment. He proposes that the relations of outer or social adjustment to affective complexity be studied thoroughly, with the expectation that some range of affective complexity will be found to be optimal for social adjustment.

The relation of affective complexity to personal or inner adjustment is more difficult to discuss, because we do not have a good definition of inner adjustment. Possibly a satisfactory definition will emerge from studies of affective complexity, flexibility, and emotional and intellectual expansion, their interrelations and their relations to the ratings given by psychiatrists and psychologists on personal adjustment as they conceive it.

This is as far as we have gone in the attempt to define and measure personal adjustment. It is not very far, but perhaps it is in the right direction. It is certainly far enough to see that the inner harmony which is personal adjustment in our society is very complex indeed.

PERSONAL AND SOCIAL ADJUSTMENT
IN RETIREMENT *Chapter XIV*

GORDON F. STREIB AND WAYNE E. THOMPSON

Gordon F. Streib, Ph.D., is assistant professor of sociology at Cornell University and director of the Study of Occupational Retirement. He is the author of articles in the field of aging and social gerontology.

Wayne E. Thompson is a research associate with the Department of Sociology and Anthropology, Cornell University, and assistant director of the Cornell Study of Occupational Retirement. He previously served as field director of this study and in that capacity contacted personally nearly 2,000 senior employees of participating organizations throughout the country.

THIS PAPER presents some preliminary findings from the In-Plant Project of the Cornell Study of Occupational Retirement.[1] Unlike the other parts of the Cornell Study and, in fact, unlike most other studies in social gerontology, the In-Plant Project is longitudinal in design; that is, it consists of repeated studies of a panel of the same subjects.

[1] The Cornell Study of Occupational Retirement is an interdisciplinary research program conducted by the Department of Sociology and Anthropology in collaboration with the Department of Rural Sociology, the School of Nutrition, and the Department of Public Health and Preventive Medicine of the Cornell Medical College in New York City. The research was made possible by funds granted by the Lilly Endowment, Inc.

The longitudinal design has a number of important advantages: [2] (1) it makes it possible to accumulate more information on the same people over a period of time; (2) types of information are obtained which are not available from a single cross-sectional study; (3) the method affords the opportunity to discern shifts in attitudes and behavior; (4) it provides a reliable method of analyzing reasons for such changes.

In the present study the participants have been contacted twice thus far. The first contact was made when the majority of the participants were approximately sixty-four years old and were gainfully employed. The second contact was made from a year to eighteen months later, at which time some participants had retired. The findings here reported are for a group of 2,007 males born in 1887, 1888, or 1889: 67 per cent or 1,338 are still gainfully employed and 669 or 33 per cent are retired. These persons reside throughout the forty-eight states, although the major concentration of participants is in the more heavily industrialized regions—New England, Middle Atlantic, and North Central. The participants are, or were, engaged in a wide variety of occupations and represent a wide range of skills, income levels, and job responsibilities. A comparison of the subjects by occupational categories shows that, with the exception of a disproportionate number of professionals, the participants approximate the distribution of the total employed male population aged sixty to sixty-four.[3]

[2] See Paul F. Lazarsfeld and Morris Rosenberg, *The Language of Social Research* (Glencoe, Illinois: The Free Press, 1955), pp. 231–59; Hans Zeisel, *Say It With Figures* (New York: Harper and Bros., 1947), pp. 211–46.

[3] It should be emphasized that while the participants are from widely diverse backgrounds, they do not constitute a representative sample of America's older population. In every case, individual par-

Much of the preliminary analysis of the In-Plant data has been directed toward answering five significant questions involved in the problem of retirement:

1. Is most retirement based on personal decision, i.e., is it voluntary, or is retirement most often externally imposed, i.e., is it compulsory?

2. Apart from compulsory retirement programs, in what respect is retirement a selective process?

3. Have the adverse effects of retirement been overestimated?

4. What is the significance of major situational factors such as economic status and physical health in adjustment to retirement?

5. What influence, if any, do preretirement attitudes play in affecting adjustment in retirement?

Let us turn to the first question.

Who decides that retirement shall occur? The findings of the present study suggest that most people who retire at the age of sixty-five come under a compulsory program. Of the participants who retired, 63 per cent did so on the basis of their "company's decision." Of course, this does not necessarily imply unwillingness on the part of the individual. As a matter of fact, 50 per cent of those who were retired under a compulsory program had a favorable attitude toward retirement and quite possibly would have retired in any case.[4]

---

ticipation has been on a voluntary basis. Moreover, co-operation by the two-hundred-odd employing organizations was voluntary, a fact which has resulted, among other things, in a disproportionate number of large, or relatively affluent organizations among those co-operating.

[4] The measure of attitude toward retirement was developed through the use of the Guttman Scaling Technique and consists of the following items:

1. "Some people say that retirement is good for a person, some say it is bad. In general, what do you think?"

In regard to the second question, whether retirement is a selective process outside of compulsory programs, our data indicate that among those who are self-retired, retirement is definitely a selective process. One important inference which we may draw from this fact is that retirement in itself may be considered as a form of adjustment to the life situation which confronts the older person in an industrialized society. Retirement is often thought to be the "end of the road"—or the "employer's scrap heap." For many people, however, this need not be the case; retirement may represent a welcome relief from the physical and psychological pressures which have become an increasing burden as the person has gotten older. In the present project, a large majority (70 per cent) of the voluntary retirants anticipated retirement with a favorable attitude. Only 29 per cent among those who did not retire were favorably disposed.

As shown in Table I, our findings indicate that both by a physician's appraisal and in their own estimation, the participants who retired voluntarily were considerably less healthy than those who continued to work.[5] Also the

---

2. "Do you mostly look forward to the time when you will stop working and retire, or in general do you dislike the idea?"
3. "If it were up to you alone, would you continue working for your present company?"

1952: Coefficient of Reproducibility = .96.
1954: Coefficient of Reproducibility = .95. (Nonretirants only)
Based on an empirically determined "cutting point," people are considered to have a favorable attitude toward retirement if they indicate they believe retirement to be mostly good for a person and in general look forward to retirement.

[5] The measure of self-health rating was developed through the use of the Guttman Scaling Technique and consists of the following items:
1. "Has your health changed during the past year?"
2. "How would you rate your health at the present time?"

(Footnotes continued on page 184.)

Table I

HEALTH AND RETIREMENT

	Percentage in Good or Excellent Health	
	People who subsequently retired voluntarily	People who continued working
Health as appraised by physicians	53 (74)[1]	72 (386)
Self-health estimate	51 (250)	69 (1338)

[1] Numbers in parentheses are the percentage bases.

people who chose to retire were significantly less satisfied with their jobs than those who continued working, and they less frequently regarded work an important value in itself. At this stage of the analysis we have not determined whether the reduced enjoyment of the job is related to decreased physical capacity for work and, perhaps, as a consequence, feelings of inferiority vis-à-vis younger workers, or whether dissatisfaction with the job reflects other relevant differences, perhaps differences in basic orientation.

As might be expected, the choice of the retirant is also affected by economic considerations. Low income appears to act as a deterrent to retirement, provided the state of health is good. In other words, if a person is in good health

3. "Do you have any particular physical or health problems at present?"
4. "Have you been seen by a doctor during the past year?"
1952: Coefficient of Reproducibility = .95.
1954: Coefficient of Reproducibility = .96.
Based on an empirically determined "cutting point," people are considered in good health if they indicate that their health has not changed, or has changed for the better, that they consider themselves in good or excellent health, and that they have no particular health problems.

and has a low income he tends to continue working rather than retire. Along these same lines, given good health, home owners are more likely to retire than are nonhome owners.

In considering the effects of retirement, we find that the panel analysis sheds light on the relationship between retirement and health. We have already indicated that poor health is an important factor which leads people to retire. Apparently this fact alone may account for the relatively larger number of persons in poor health among retirants, for we do not find that retirement leads to poor health. As shown in Table II, the retired and the nonretired do

Table II
CHANGES IN HEALTH

Percentage of People Whose Health Was Good When Contacted Initially		
	Retirants	Nonretirants
Percentage whose health worsened	25	22
Percentage whose health remained good	75	78
	100 (382)	100 (926)

Percentage of People Whose Health Was Poor When Contacted Initially		
	Retirants	Nonretirants
Percentage whose health improved	36	37
Percentage whose health remained poor	64	63
	100 (287)	100 (412)

not differ significantly in the proportion whose health improved, worsened, or remained the same. Our findings are thus consistent with the recent study reported by Robert J. Myers, who employed statistics from both public and private pension plans. Myers wrote:

It seems likely that this higher mortality in the early years of retirement arises from the fact that those in poorer health are more apt to retire at or shortly after the minimum retirement age, while the healthier individuals continue at work.[6]

Not only does it appear that retirement has no deleterious effect on health, but also, using as an index of adjustment our measure of dejection, there are no significant increases in poor adjustment among those who retire.[7]

Reading Table III horizontally we note that in 1952 approximately the same percentage of persons (about 25

Table III

COMPARISON OF RETIRED AND WORKING RESPONDENTS
ON DEJECTION SCALE IN 1952 AND 1954

	Retirants (669 cases) Percentage Dejected		*Nonretirants* (1,338 cases) Percentage Dejected	
	Much	Little	Much	Little
1952	28	72	25	75
1954	25	75	23	77

per cent) in both groups—those who subsequently retired and those who continued working—were poorly adjusted.

[6] Robert J. Myers, "Factors in Interpreting Mortality After Retirement," *Journ. Amer. Statis. Assoc.*, 49 (1954): 508.

[7] The measure of dejection was developed through the use of the Guttman Scaling Technique and consists of the following items:
1. "How often do you get the feeling that your life today is not very useful?"
2. "How often do you find yourself feeling 'blue'?"
3. "How often do you get upset by the things that happen in your day-to-day living?"

1952: Coefficient of Reproducibility = .96.
1954: Coefficient of Reproducibility = .95.
Based on an empirically determined "cutting point," people are considered not to be dejected if they indicate that they hardly ever feel life is not very useful and that they hardly ever feel "blue."

Perhaps even more interesting, however, is the fact that at the time of the second contact in 1954, the percentage of poorly adjusted in both groups remained at about the same level. In other words, when we compare those persons who subsequently retired with those who continued working we note no difference in the proportion who are well adjusted.

Does the over-all picture which has just been presented oversimplify what happens in adjustment to retirement versus continued employment? It must be admitted that the whole story is not told by one statistical table; there is much more that must be known. Indeed, within the longitudinal design it is possible to probe further and to ask a more specific and more challenging type of question. Granted that there are no differences in the over-all adjustment of retirants versus those still employed, how about the internal change or turnover within the subgroup? That is, do the adjusted within the two occupational groups remain adjusted through time or are there shifts? It is possible that some persons who are well adjusted before retirement may become poorly adjusted, and the reverse may occur. Turning to the data in Table IV, we find a remarkable consistency in terms of turnover when we compare the retired with those who are still working. First, let us look at the two columns labeled "Good Adjustment."

In both the retired and the working group the overwhelming percentage of persons who were well adjusted remained well adjusted. Only about one in six of those who were rated as good in adjustment shifted to poor. On the other hand, we find that among the 1952 poor adjustment group there has been much more turnover, but we note that this change has been in the direction of improvement. About half the persons in the poor adjustment group

Table IV

COMPARISON OF THE RETIRED VERSUS WORKING
RESPONDENTS ON MEASURE OF ADJUSTMENT,
ACCORDING TO 1952 DEGREE OF ADJUSTMENT

	Retirants 1952		*Nonretirants* 1952	
	Poor Adjustment (187)	Good Adjustment (482)	Poor Adjustment (334)	Good Adjustment (1,004)
1954 Percentage with poor adjustment	46	17	52	13
Percentage with good adjustment	54	83	48	87

in 1952 were rated as good adjustment in 1954. And the point which we would like to emphasize is that as great an improvement in adjustment took place among those who subsequently retired as among those who continued to work. These data suggest that the adverse effects of retirement have indeed been overestimated.

There is considerable discussion and some evidence in the field of social gerontology which supports the idea that retirement leads to maladjustment. The basic assumption which lies behind this point of view is that in an industrialized society, such as our own, the cultural standards and values emphasize the importance of work. Indeed some observers have referred to the United States as a work-centered culture. In regard to occupational retirement, this point of view implies that there is no role which is an adequate or satisfactory substitute for the worker role.

A number of published empirical studies offer preliminary evidence that there is a higher incidence of poor personal adjustment among retirants than among persons who continue working.[8] The picture is not clear-cut, however, for there is practically an equal amount of evidence indicating that a large number of retirants, in some cases a majority of the sample involved, are very well adjusted.[9]

The point has been well phrased by Friedmann and Havighurst, who wrote: "The temptation is strong to imply that, because the worker has found added significance in his job, depriving him of it through compulsory retirement—even with adequate income—would represent a grave social injustice. *No such case can be made in any categorical fashion on the basis of our findings.*[10] (Italics theirs.)

The preliminary findings of the Cornell longitudinal study indicated that by far the greatest proportion of the people who retired were well adjusted during the period under investigation. Using a number of specific measures

[8] See, for example, Joseph H. Britton, "The Personal Adjustment of Retired School Teachers," *Journ. Gerontol.*, 8 (1953): 333–38.

Jean O. Britton and Joseph H. Britton, "Factors Related to the Adjustment of YMCA Secretaries," *ibid.*, 6 (1951): 34–38.

Robert J. Havighurst and Ethel Shanas, "Retirement and the Professional Worker," *ibid.*, 8 (1953): 81–85.

Judson T. Landis, "Social-Psychological Factors of Aging," *Social Forces*, 20 (1942): 460–67.

[9] See, for example, Joseph H. Britton and Jean O. Britton, "Work and Retirement for Older University Alumni," *Journ. Gerontol.*, 9 (1954): 468–74.

L. C. Michelon, "The New Leisure Class," *Amer. Journ. Sociology*, 59 (1954): 371–78.

David O. Moberg, "Church Membership and Personal Adjustment in Old Age," *Journ. Gerontol.*, 8 (1953): 207–11.

Special Surveys, *They Tell About Retirement: A Special Survey of Retired Men in Cleveland* (Cleveland, Ohio: Special Surveys, 1952).

[10] Eugene A. Friedmann and R. J. Havighurst, *The Meaning of Work and Retirement* (Chicago: University of Chicago Press, 1954), p. 186.

of adjustment in retirement we found that a large proportion of the subjects are making a satisfactory adjustment. On the measure of dissatisfaction with retirement, we found that 72 per cent are relatively satisfied with retirement.[11] On items ascertaining the "effects" of retirement, 67 per cent said that retirement has none of the negative effects included, whereas only 5 per cent mentioned all of the negative effects.[12] On still another item—the question: "How difficult have you found not working?"—only 15 per cent indicated that they have found not working very difficult; 65 per cent said they have not found it difficult at all.

If we accept the finding that retirement may not have disastrous effects for all retirants, we are prepared to move on to the analytical task of determining what factors are correlated with adjustment in the retirant role. In other

[11] The measure of dissatisfaction with retirement was developed through the use of the Guttman Scaling Technique and consists of the following items:
1. "How often do you miss being with other people at work?"
2. "How often do you miss the feeling of doing a good job?"
3. "How often do you worry about not having a job?"
4. "How often do you feel that you want to go back to work?"
Coefficient of Reproducibility = .97.
Based on an empirically determined "cutting point," people are considered to be "satisfied" with retirement if they indicate that they hardly ever feel they want to return to work, hardly ever worry about not having a job, and hardly ever miss the feeling of doing a good job.

[12] The measure of negative appraisal of the effects of retirement was developed through the use of the Guttman Scaling Technique and consists of the following items:
1. "Do you think that stopping work has given you the feeling that your life today is not very useful?"
2. "Do you think that stopping work has made you less satisfied with your way of life today?"
3. "Do you think that stopping work has made you think of yourself as older or younger?"
Coefficient of Reproducibility = .96.

words, is it possible to determine, even in a crude fashion, what factors facilitate good adjustment? Here we shall examine some of the data which will offer at least a tentative answer to our third question: What is the significance of major situational factors like economic status and physical health in adjustment to retirement?

A basic assumption of our research at Cornell is that physical, mental, social, and economic aspects of a person's life are highly interrelated.[13]

At the present time there is, unfortunately, no adequate empirical technique for dealing simultaneously with the complex factors which affect personal adjustment. We can hope, however, that as more time, thought, and attention are given to the field, useful theoretical models will be developed which are utilizable in empirical research.

There seems to be fairly wide agreement that two basic variables related to adjustment are physical health and reduced income. Indeed, empirical studies have established quite conclusively that both ill health[14] and low socio-economic status[15] are positively related to poor adjustment among older persons. Our preliminary analysis of the Cornell data seems to show that health and socio-economic status must be regarded as basic in any analysis. Let us see how these two variables are related to adjustment.

If we utilize two measures of adjustment—a dejection

[13] A similar assumption is made, of course, by other investigators. See, for example, Ernest W. Burgess, "The Role of Sociology," in *Health in the Later Years,* ed. John M. Maclachlan (Gainesville: University of Florida Press, 1953), p. 34.

[14] See, for example, Britton, *op. cit.,* Britton and Britton, *op. cit.,* Landis, *op. cit.,* and R. J. Havighurst and Ruth Albrecht, *Older People* (New York: Longmans Green and Co., 1953).

[15] See, for example, Britton and Britton, *op. cit.,* and Havighurst and Albrecht, *op. cit.*

scale [16] and a scale measuring satisfaction with life—[17] we find that adjustment is clearly related to a situational factor such as physical and health condition—both before and after retirement. As is shown in Table V, differences in excess of 40 per cent, which is well beyond the required level for statistical significance, were found when we compared those people who were in good health and those who were in poor health. Among those in poor health, one-half the persons may be classified as poorly adjusted, as compared to approximately one person in ten among those in good health. This was true for the group who subsequently retired, and also for those who were still actively employed.

Similarly, economic considerations have an important effect on the adjustment of the individual. Among both those who retired and those who continued working, dejection and dissatisfaction with life were inversely correlated with the amount of income received. And this same pattern—the higher the income, the less the dejection and dissatisfaction—appeared before and after retirement.

To be sure, objective income provides only an approximate measure of the adequacy of the individual's economic resources. Of equal importance is the individual's

---

[16] See footnote 7.

[17] The measure of satisfaction with life was developed through the use of the Guttman Scaling Technique and consists of the following items:

1. "All in all, how much happiness would you say you find in life today?"
2. "In general, how would you say you feel most of the time, in good spirits or in low spirits?"
3. "On the whole, how satisfied would you say you are with your way of life today?"

Coefficient of Reproducibility = .96.

In 1954, the item of happiness was worded differently, but a score consisting of the other two items provides a comparable measure of satisfaction with life.

Table V

THE RELATION OF HEALTH AND TWO MEASURES OF
ADJUSTMENT FOR THE PANEL MEMBERS WHO ARE
RETIRED AND THOSE STILL EMPLOYED

	Retirants		*Nonretirants*	
	Poor Health	Good Health	Poor Health	Good Health
First Measure (1952)	(287)[1]	(382)	(412)	(926)
Percentage dejected	58	15	50	21
Percentage dissatisfied with life	54	8	50	9
Second Measure (1954)	(281)	(388)	(454)	(884)
Percentage dejected	46	10	53	14
Percentage dissatisfied with life	47	9	39	6

[1] Numbers within the parentheses are the percentage base.

own appraisal of the adequacy of his income. This evaluation is an expression of the individual's values in given situational contexts: thus, it varies with the individual and with the situation. For this reason, although income and feelings of economic deprivation are highly correlated, the latter measure is probably the more meaningful in studies of adjustment and readjustment. This probability is substantiated empirically by the fact that dejection and dissatisfaction are more closely related to feelings of economic deprivation than to objective income.

Clearly, retirement is practically synonymous with a reduction in income. But to the extent that the values of the retirant change with a change in his life situation, such a reduction income, at least hypothetically, does not necessarily mean an increase in economic deprivation. In point of fact, however, economic deprivation does increase following retirement, but primarily among those who retire unwillingly. This, of course, points up the importance of personal values in making the adjustment to retirement.

Nevertheless, these findings, when coupled with those previously reported, underscore the point that it is not the impact of retirement alone which results in poor adjustment but retirement plus massive situational factors like health and socio-economic status which are crucial to adjustment, and which may affect adjustment in a significant fashion before retirement as well as afterward.

In conclusion, let us turn to the last question which was raised at the outset: What influence, if any, do preretirement attitudes have on adjustment in retirement?

In our work at Cornell we have come to rely rather heavily on the concept of anticipatory retirement [18] for interpreting many of our findings. Implicit in this concept is the idea that retirement is not merely a state of being retired but may more properly be considered as a process which goes on over a period of time and only ultimately may lead to a state of being retired. When retirement is viewed from this perspective, it is clear that problems pertaining to adjustment in retirement do not necessarily arise only after the employee has stopped work. They may precede retirement by a considerable period of time. At the start of the Cornell longitudinal study, we selected persons who were sixty-four years of age because we thought that this was the age prior to the most common chronological retirement age, sixty-five. We now think, however, along with other investigators in this field, such as Clark Tibbitts and Harold Jones, that one must go back earlier in the life cycle, perhaps to age fifty or fifty-five

[18] This is a special case of the phenomenon of anticipatory socialization. See Robert K. Merton and Alice S. Kitt, "Contributions to the Theory of Reference Group Behavior," in *Continuities in Social Research,* ed. Robert K. Merton and Paul F. Lazarsfeld (Glencoe, Illinois: The Free Press, 1950), p. 87ff.

and even earlier, to assess more specifically what a person's adjustment to retirement will be.

Our findings clearly point to the conclusion that attitude and behavior prior to retirement have a very definite relationship to adjustment in retirement. We find, for example, that approximately one-third of the persons who had a preretirement attitude unfavorable toward retirement are dissatisfied with retirement. On the other hand, among those whose preretirement attitude was favorable toward retirement, only 6 per cent were dissatisfied with retirement. This finding takes on greater significance if we again recall that the study is a longitudinal one and the preretirement attitude was determined at least a year in advance of the actual retirement. Therefore we are not relying on the respondents' memories as to how they felt about retirement before it happened.

The importance of a person's preconception of retirement can also be shown by other data relating to dissatisfaction with retirement. It has been mentioned that the feeling of economic deprivation is important in determining how one regards retirement. People who have a negative attitude toward retirement before retiring, however, tend to be dissatisfied with retirement, regardless of whether they feel economically deprived. Negative anticipation of retirement appears to be a stronger influence than the feeling of economic deprivation. It appears that W. I. Thomas' proposition may have some validity in such situations, for, it will be recalled, he said that if men conceive situations as real, they are real in their consequences. It appears that if a person has a negative orientation toward retirement it may even overcome the fact that he does not feel economically deprived. An obvious practical implication of such a finding is that the provision of adequate economic security is undoubtedly of great importance in facilitating adjustment in old age and during retirement. But there is still a great need to educate, in the broadest sense of the term, persons who have a negative orientation toward retirement.

The importance of the preretirement attitude toward retirement as a factor influencing satisfaction in retirement is also shown by Table VI. Three variables which are often thought to be important—having plans for retirement, expecting to retire, and retiring voluntarily—are of little significance in contributing to satisfaction with retirement, given the same attitude toward retirement. More specifically, satisfaction with retirement is not related to whether retirement has been voluntary or involuntary, provided the retirants have the same anticipatory attitude.

Among those who had a favorable attitude, having plans apparently is conducive in a minor way to satisfaction in retirement; however, here also the great differences are between those who had a favorable attitude and those who did not. In short, plans, expectations, and who makes the decision, are of little consequence regarding satisfaction with retirement—given the same preretirement attitude.

In summary, to review these preliminary findings from the In-Plant Project of the Cornell Study of Occupational Retirement:

1. Most of the participants who retired at sixty-five did so under compulsory programs.
2. For persons not under compulsory retirement programs, retirement is a selective process, such retirement being a product of a variously arrived-at favorable attitude toward retirement, poor health, dissatisfaction with the job, and a relatively favorable economic position.

Table VI

SATISFACTION WITH RETIREMENT AS THE RESULT OF
ATTITUDE TOWARD RETIREMENT

	Percentage Who Are Satisfied With Retirement	
	Favorable Preretirement Attitude Toward Retirement	Unfavorable Preretirement Attitude Toward Retirement
Have plans	86 (183) [1]	61 (82)
Do not have plans	77 (202)	58 (202)
Self-retired	83 (174)	66 (76)
Company-retired	80 (211)	56 (208)
Expected to retire	82 (354)	60 (171)
Expected to continue working	68 (31)	57 (113)

[1] Numbers in parentheses are the percentage bases.

3. There is convincing evidence that there may be an overestimation of the adverse effects of retirement, although this conclusion is obviously limited by the population being studied.

4. As other investigators have shown, the major situational factors of good health and high socio-economic status are fundamental in aiding good adjustment in old age, both before and after retirement.

5. Perhaps the most important predictor of whether a person will make a satisfactory adjustment to retirement is his preretirement attitude toward retirement.

As we have indicated, these findings are based on the very early phases of analysis of the data, and for this reason they should be considered suggestive, not conclusive. They do, however, point the way for our own subsequent investigation—and, we hope, for other investigators as well.

EMERGING PRINCIPLES
AND CONCEPTS:
A SUMMARY *Chapter XV*

WILMA DONAHUE

Wilma Donahue, Ph.D., is research psychologist and chairman of the Division of Gerontology, Institute for Human Adjustment, and lecturer in psychology at the University of Michigan. She is the author of numerous publications relating to the field of gerontology and editor of the books Earning Opportunities for Older Workers, Housing the Aging, Education for Later Maturity *and of several others. At present Dr. Donahue is also serving as chairman of the Multi-University Sponsored Training Institute in Social Gerontology.*

THE AGING of the American population is a relatively recent event. While the underlying factors became operative during the nineteenth century, the appearance of a large element of retired older persons did not occur until well into the present century. The customary lag between rapid social change and its systematic study has given rise to misconceptions regarding the nature of this new segment of the population and its relationship to the whole.

Many people, professional and lay alike, share the belief that the proportion of older persons in the population will double during the next generation or two and that as a consequence they will become an insuperable burden on the economy. There are also the widespread beliefs, in opposition to each other, that most older people are doomed to a prolonged state of invalidism and that the older age group contains a large and eager labor reserve up to at least twice the number of older persons currently employed. It is frequently asserted that retirement from work, particularly if it is compulsory, hastens death. And there are many who hold that all older people desire constant association with young people and that adult children who refuse to provide housing, financial support, and companionship for their aged parents are morally decayed.

When these beliefs are examined in the light of emerging research findings none is found to have more than a modicum of validity. Moreover, widespread adherence to such erroneous stereotyped ideas is almost certainly retarding progress in meeting the real needs of older persons and giving rise to some unsound programs. Recognition of these facts suggested the desirability of bringing together a number of scientists who have been doing research on some of the fundamental questions involved and asking them to set forth their conclusions in unmistakable language.

The preceding chapters present a number of principles and concepts which have emerged from the work of these students. Some of their conclusions are at variance with current opinion and some suggest approaches that call for departure from traditional values and modes of behavior. Others represent preliminary results and serve the purpose of pointing the way toward further and more refined researches.

Another obstacle in reaching a body of sound knowledge about the phenomenon of aging and about older people is that much of the research and program planning is segmented. False or partial conclusions are frequently reached by reason of the failure to examine the total situation or person or to relate the findings of a particular investigation to those of other studies that impinge upon the immediate problem at hand. The plan of bringing together a number of scientists from different though related fields represented an effort to achieve some integration of the newer knowledge of aging. The summary which follows attempts to reflect some of the exchange of ideas and concepts that took place among the investigators who participated in the symposium. Because of this effort at synthesis, specific identification of some points with the prepared papers is lost. The major part of the summary, however, is derived from these presentations. Some pertinent data from equally reliable sources have been introduced.

Population Trends

Projections of the number of older people and of their relative importance in the population are of interest because of their significance for the economy as a whole, for the size of the labor force, and for planning in such fields as housing, education, recreation, and health and welfare services. Conservative estimates of the future numbers of older persons are relatively easy to forecast. Persons who will be sixty-five years of age in 1975 are now in middle age and those who will be sixty-five in the year 2000 are now in their late teens. Thus, by applying current mortality rates to appropriate age groups in the present population, it may be predicted that today's older population of fourteen million will increase to about twenty-one million by 1975 and to twenty-seven million by 2000. The somewhat smaller increase during the last quarter of the century is attributable to the temporary decline in the number of births during the 1930's.

By using the same technique, it may be forecast that the middle-aged population between forty-five and sixty-four years of age will climb from thirty-four million in 1955 to forty-three million by 1975 and to at least fifty-three million by the year 2000.

One of the well-known characteristics of the older population is the disproportionate number of women which arises as a consequence of their greater capacity for survival. On the assumption that the present differential will continue, the 1975 older population will have approximately twelve million women and nine million men. And the older population at the turn of the century may consist of sixteen million women and about eleven million men.

These large numerical increases reflect the increase in the size of the total population more than anything else and the saving of lives in the younger age groups. The current rising number of births and more rapid increases in life expectancy in the earlier years result in more people at all ages. Thus the anticipated increases in the proportion of older persons in the population are much less dramatic. Older people today account for about 8.5 per cent of the United States population. This ratio is expected to rise to between 9.5 per cent and 10.5 per cent by 1975 and probably to level off at somewhere around the higher figure during the last quarter of the century.

There is the possibility, of course, that the marked increase in research on long-term illness and on the aging process itself will give rise to more rapid extension of life in the older years. Mortality rates among persons up to age eighty-five years are showing considerable declines. In consequence, average length of life at age sixty has risen about three years since 1900 and may show a further increase of two years by 1975. Past and projected increases in length of life remaining at age forty-five are somewhat greater, indicating more progress in reduction of mortality among people in the middle years than among those in the later years of life. The conservative conclusion is, therefore, that the more immediate benefits of research and improved health and medical procedures are likely to be measured in terms of more people living through the middle years and entering the older years as healthier and more effective individuals rather than in any marked extension of life in the advanced ages.

Health Improvements

Striking improvements in the health of older people can be effected through application of knowledge already available. One of the important factors is to develop an effective regard for the individual as a total person and to take cognizance of the psychological and social aspects of his nature along with the purely biological. There is now ample evidence of the two-way relationship between health and the satisfaction of needs for social recognition, useful activity, and meaningful human relationships.

Long periods of helplessness and institutionalization are not seen as a necessary consequence of the further extension of life into the later years. It is being well demonstrated in Great Britain and increasingly in the United States that application of the whole man principle together with complete therapeutic and restorative services enables the vast majority of old people to live in the community independently or with a minimum of supportive services. Quite beyond the experimental stage is the pattern of the geriatric diagnostic-treatment-restorative center as part of a constellation of facilities including community housing, congregate living facilities, social and work centers, vacations, and, when needed, housekeeping help, nursing service, day hospital care, meals delivered to the home, and friendly visiting. And a *sine qua non* is the integration of public and private programs with a central information, guidance, and referral facility in order that their services may be brought to bear promptly as individual circumstances require.

Psychological Function

Basically, it must be stated without much mincing of words that most mental capacities deteriorate along with the physical as years accumulate. This statement does not say, however, that the capacity to enjoy life as a participating, useful member of the community is destroyed. What is implied, rather, is that the middle-aged or older individual who wishes to live life fully will (like individuals of any age) take stock of his assets and losses and choose his activities accordingly.

There is an appreciable accumulation of scientific evidence in this area. While persons of sixty may cope less well with novel situations than they did in earlier years, they appear to be approximately as capable in terms of knowledge and understanding of verbal materials as they were at the age of nineteen or twenty. Certainly, there are hundreds of older persons who are quite successfully refreshing earlier skills and developing interests they were forced to set aside during their busier years. They are demonstrating the basic principle that capability is translated into performance only to the extent that the individual takes the initiative in finding ways to keep himself alert and functional. Research has also underpinned the common observation that there are vast differences among older people in their capacities for performance of all kinds of tasks.

Employment and Leisure

There are also clearly measurable trends in the changing distribution of the adult years between gainful employment and leisure time. By reason of longer life and the great increase in productivity, people are at once contributing more years to the work force and at the same time devoting a smaller proportion of their lives to it. Because more people are living into and through the productive years, average work life expectancy has risen to forty-two years, an increase of a full ten years since 1900. Further increase is anticipated by reason of improving health status and of the projected increase in life expectancy of young adults and of middle-aged persons.

Simultaneously, continued shortening of the work week and the persistent trend toward earlier retirement from work are giving more leisure to all workers and more years of complete leisure to those who survive into the later years. Of all men sixty-five years of age and over, 60 per cent are retired in contrast to about 30 per cent in 1900. By 1975 retirement from work to other forms of activity may claim 70 per cent of the older men.

Despite the improvement in health mentioned earlier, ill-health and declining energy still appear to be the major factor in bringing about retirement from the work force. Several careful surveys indicate that the population over age sixty-five contains a relatively small number of persons who feel able to or are interested in returning to full-time employment. Broad extension of opportunity for part-time work or for sheltered employment might alter the picture considerably.

During the current decade the needs of the economy may create ten million additional jobs. Demographic and retirement trends indicate that approximately one-half of these will have to be filled by middle-aged men and women, with women filling the major proportion. Thus, it becomes clear that employment policies will have to make still further adjustment to the changing age profile of the population and that even more women will enter paid employment as they complete their parental responsibilities.

Simultaneously, the rise in leisure calls for rapid extension of facilities for liberal adult education, for self-expression in the fine arts and in the artcrafts, for recreation, and for opportunity for older people to serve the community through voluntary activities and citizenship roles.

Retirement Income and the Economy

It was stated at the outset that many who observe the rising number of older people jump quickly to the conclusion that they will shortly impose a drain on the economy of sufficient magnitude to undermine the standard of living of the whole population. This hasty conclusion completely overlooks the record during the first half of the century over which period the standard of living increased two-and-one-half times while the older population increased four-and-one-half times. It ignores the great rise in development and applications of machines and mechanical energy, in reinvestment in production facilities, in the extension of work-life expectancy mentioned heretofore, and the long-time decline in the proportion of children. Continuation of current trends in productivity, in investment in capital goods, in work-life expectancy, and in participation of women in paid employment would seem to provide a basis for removing the fear of any disastrous effect of a larger number of older people on the economy. Indeed, a number of economists have vouchsafed the observation that the future population of older people can be assured of financial security, of adequate health services, housing, and educational and recreational opportunities without in any way jeopardizing the general level of living.

Family Relationships

One of the basic changes in the American culture has been the trend toward separation of the family generations and the greater individuation of the family members. The large kinship group in which all members contributed to the multi-faceted household enterprise, under the direction of the older members, developed out of the agrarian, craft culture that preceded mechanization of agricultural, manufacturing, and household tasks. The household has broken down into its components of one-generation and two-generation family units because these smaller groups are more adaptable to urban industrial, mobile society. There is growing evidence that most couples are as eager to retain their independence after their children have grown up as their children are to have them do so. Even the majority of truly aged report that they feel more comfortable in having their own incomes from Social Security and elsewhere, thus being able to associate with their peers and not having to impose upon their children. The support members of all age groups are giving to public programs for older people and the individual responsibilities many adult children are assuming on behalf of their parents would seem to indicate rising rather than declining concern.

It appears that the new normal intergeneration relationship is based on mutual respect, friendship, and reciprocal helpfulness when opportunity arises.

INDEX